# A SAFE HOUSE

OTHER BOOKS BY MARIA JACOBS

*Precautions Against Death* (poems and prose). Mosaic Press, Oakville, ON, 1983.

*Vijfenvijftig Sokken: Het dagelijks leven met onderduikers in de tweede wereldoorlog.* De Harmonie, Amsterdam. 1983.

*The Third Taboo: A collection of poems on jealousy* (co-edited with Heather Cadsby). Wolsak and Wynn Publishers Ltd., Toronto, ON, 1983.

*With Other Words: A Bilingual Anthology of Contemporary Dutch Poetry by Women* (editor and translator). Netherlandic Press, Windsor, ON, 1985.

*What Feathers Are For* (poems). Mosaic Press, Oakville, ON, 1986.

*Iseult, We Are Barren* (poems). Netherlandic Press, Windsor, ON, 1987.

*Dutch Gifts: Stories, Poems and Creative Non-Fiction on a Netherlandic Theme* (editor). Netherlandic Press, Windsor, ON, 1991.

# A
# SAFE
# ◧ HOUSE ◨

HOLLAND 1940–1945

*Maria Jacobs*

MARIA JACOBS

SERAPHIM EDITIONS

Copyright © Maria Jacobs 2005

All rights reserved. No part of this publication may be reproduced or transmitted in any form or by any means – electronic or mechanical, including photocopying, recording or any information storage and retrieval system – without written permission from the publisher, except by a reviewer who wishes to quote brief passages for inclusion in a review.

Library and Archives Canada Cataloguing in Publication

Jacobs, Maria, 1930–
[Precautions against death]
    A safe house : Holland, 1940-1945 / Maria Jacobs.

First published under title: Precautions against death.
ISBN 0-9734588-5-2

1. World War, 1939-1945 – Netherlands – Amersfoort – Poetry. 2. World War, 1939-1945 – Jews – Rescue – Netherlands – Amersfoort – Poetry. 3. World War, 1939-1945 – Personal narratives, Dutch. I. Title.

PS8569.A289P74 2005    C811'.54    C2005-902800-9

Editor: Allan Briesmaster
Cover and Interior Design: Marijke Friesen
Cover Photos: Photographers unknown; photo of rubble and troops from the private collection of Maureen Whyte; photo of the house from the private collection of the author
Author Photograph: Richard Lush

Parts of this book were published as *Precautions Against Death* in 1983 by Mosaic Press, Oakville.

Poems in this book have previously appeared in the following publications:
*Canadian Journal of Netherlandic Studies* (in Dutch and French translation); *CV II*; *Intrinsic*; *Opzij* (in Dutch translation); *Waves*; *What Feathers Are For*; *Iseult*, *We Are Barren*; and *A Discord of Flags*.

Most of the poems were first broadcast by CJRT-FM.

A group of twenty poems were featured on Robert Weaver's CBC Radio programme *Anthology*.

The publisher gratefully acknowledges the financial assistance of The Canada Council for the Arts.

Printed and bound in Canada

Seraphim Editions
238 Emerald Street North
Hamilton, Ontario
Canada L8L 5K8
info@seraphimeditions.com

This book is dedicated to the memory of my mother, Lucie Wolsak, and to the memory of all those who slept, for one night or for many, under the roof of her safe house.

# A SAFE HOUSE

HEAVY WEATHER AHEAD

"Listen," she said, "I have to tell you this. Dad and I have decided to separate." I was about seven, and my mother and I were walking along the quiet suburban street where we lived.
"When?"
"Pretty soon. He's going out to sea again. When he comes back he will stay with aunt Mol and Uncle Jaap until he finds a place of his own."
"Will you get married again?" I asked.
"Never!" she said, without hesitation.
When I had thought about it for a while I concluded that the separation would not make much difference to us. My father had been a captain in the merchant marine for as long as I could remember – eleven months out, one month home. And since my mother had said she would never marry again, what would change? But still, I remember exactly what the fence we walked beside looked like, the way the grass grew at

the curb, the green algae on one side of the trees at the intersection we had just passed when she told me.

At first I seemed to have been right. My mother, my older brother Wil, and I went on living together as we had always done. Wil and I continued to play, have our tiffs, make up, and play again. The only difference was that when my father's ship put in, we visited him onboard ship as though he were a kind uncle who gave us a good time for a couple of days now and then, and who did not shout at us, or send us to bed, as our father had done on occasion.

A year or so later, when my father was about to join his ship in Rotterdam, he came to get me to spend a day with him in that city. It was only a month or so before the Nazi bombardment laid waste to Rotterdam's core, so he was just in time to show me the new zoo and take me out for dinner in a restaurant. When he put me on the train to go back home to Amersfoort where I lived, he gave me one of his famous bear hugs – much growling and show of violence, but really more like the hug of an eiderdown blanket.

When he kissed me goodbye he tried to look cheerful, but for an instant I felt something of the pain he must have felt in leaving us for God only knew how long: he could see the storm brewing and knew he could not stick around to navigate for the Nazis. Through a screen of dancing and shaking sparkles I saw him, saw part of myself, shrinking, vanishing with the receding platform. An old lady gave me a clean blue-edged handkerchief and left me to compose myself before starting a chat.

My mother was waiting for me at the railway station in Amersfoort. Leaning out of the train window I saw her at once, though she was small and the platform was crowded. The anxious look on her pretty round face made up for the loss of my father in Rotterdam. I vowed to hold on to her, tight and for always. The war made me honour my vow.

EVACUATION

The war was inevitable. Hitler's *Realpolitik* necessitated control of the Atlantic seaboard and for that he had to have Holland, Belgium, and France, and on 10 May 1940 the German troops invaded the country.

We lived on the south side of a small park. To the west lay a tract of woodland with shrub oak and young beeches, and in these bushes a trench had hastily been dug and a battery of large cannons installed to defend the town and stop the troops approaching from the east.

As the enemy advanced it was thought that our city would become a major battlefield and the city council decided to proceed to evacuation. We could bring an overnight case and food for one day. My mother first packed, and then she prepared one last midday meal: macaroni with cheese and tomatoes. When we had finished we left the plates and dishes with the orange remains of our dinner on the table and pulled the door shut behind us.

We had to gather in the park, where we were given a number and were told to which group we belonged, city block by city block, and who would be our group leader. We waited for the command to start marching to the station where trains would take us to the north of Holland. At one point, my brother went to talk with some friends, and my mother, having lost sight of him, became almost hysterical and shrieked, "Don't leave yet; my son, my son is lost! Has anyone seen my son?" He came back in a minute, and after that I don't think my mother lost her head again, not even when the firing started. A sergeant had come to warn us and told us to keep our mouths open and stop our ears. Though the projectiles passed over our heads, we looked right into the muzzles and the flash and thunder of the cannon were alarming.

Much later we made it to the station and were packed tightly in trains which took 12 hours to get us to the north of Holland, ordinarily a three-hour trip. As we went along it became clear that part of Holland's defence consisted of opening locks and flooding farmland, so that we seemed to pass through lake after lake in the half-light of the early morning. Houses stood empty and dark with water up to their windows.

When we arrived at our destination everything was so well organised that it seemed as though every move had been rehearsed for months: we were billeted, city block by city block, in a series of small villages straggling along a highway. Dislocations had been kept to a minimum so that our neighbours in Amersfoort were billeted next door to us. My friend Marion and I didn't lose a single day's play.

The name of "our" village was Nieuweniedorp, which means something like New Newton, and Marion and I discussed this odd name at length while trying to catch frogs in the flowering field across the road. We really had wanted to play with our tops, which were all the rage just then. They looked like little mushrooms and were made of wood stained in solid colours – purple, yellow, blue-green, and cyclamen – and we decorated them with gold or silver thumbtacks and painted circles in contrasting colours around the tacks. We thought the effect was stunning when the tops were spinning. Our fathers' old shoelaces, tied to sticks, made good whips, though the laces wore out fast and came off the sticks frequently, so that we spent more time keeping our equipment in order than in actual play. But now both work and play with the tops were out, since the street in front of our hosts' house was made of pink bricks rather than the smooth asphalt of our suburban streets at home, and in any case, the tops did not make the trip with us. So we had to make do with the frogs near the ditch in a field full of buttercups and dandelions. The sun shone every day – it was a spring to end all springs.

THE NAZIS TAKE OVER

The war as well as the evacuation lasted five days. When the Germans had laid the centre of Rotterdam in ruins killing hundreds, and threatened to do the same to all the other major cities in Holland, the Government had no option but to capitulate. When the news reached us my mother cried. But on our trip back to Amersfoort she confronted her first German soldiers with her chin up and her mouth shut, her eyes dry. Back home nothing much seemed to have happened. The fighting had stopped short of the town. The firing of the cannons had blown out some of our windows but no one had entered our wide-open house and the first thing we did was scrape the mouldy remains of our macaroni off the plates.

At first life seemed to go on pretty well as usual: the milkman came, school started again, and Marion and I dug up our tops and gave them a new array of pastel circles. The early summer flowers bloomed in our gardens as if the war did not concern them. Only the foreign soldiers marching loudly through our streets, whistling and singing *Lili Marlehn* and *Wir Fahren Gegen Engeland,* reminded us of the change. One day I came home in tears because I had seen how one German soldier had been pulled out of the ranks by a sergeant for breaking stride, and was made to run around the troop in circles while the other soldiers kept right on marching. Each time the sergeant could reach him he kicked the culprit and hit him with his crop to go faster. What had upset me most was the apparent indifference on the faces of his marching comrades who did not avert their glance from a point in the distance ahead of them. My mother said, "If they do that to their own, can you imagine what they do to their prisoners?" She said it more to herself than to me, for this was the beginning and I hadn't seen the prisoners yet.

But my mother knew more and saw more. She read the *Bekanntmachungen* posted in town by the *Ortskommandant,* and learned exactly what was expected of the citizenry. One of the first things we had to do was hand in our radio sets, because the Germans did not want us to hear the short-wave newscasts from England. Every radio-owner in the country used to pay a listening fee in those days and each set was registered, so there were lists and all the Germans had to do was to come to the house and claim the set. Ours was a shiny deluxe model, a brown-flecked Bakelite egg-shaped apparatus with a round slatted speaker covered with beige raw silk, and two knobs with a fan-shaped window in between that glowed amber when the set was turned on, and had an indicator showing the frequencies. It had always seemed to me that our radio had a face, like Humpty Dumpty, and I liked it. When the soldiers came and took it away it almost felt as though they were taking a member of the family into custody.

Next came instructions about copper, brass, silver, and pewter. All items made of these metals were to be handed over. Even aside from the fact that our only riches consisted of just these items – a few antique kettles and pots, pewter pitchers and platters, and some table silver – my mother knew that the metals were needed to make guns and ammunition and decided she was not going to help. She and Will packed everything in old rags and stuffed the smaller items inside one large copper boiler she used by the hearth to store firewood. This was wrapped in more rags, and then in a large piece of blue and white chequered oilcloth that used to be put on the dining room table when we were small. Wil dug a deep hole in our back yard near the woodshed and the whole kit and caboodle was buried and stayed there for the remainder of the war. When the soldiers came to round up the metal my mother gave them two brass planters and six pewter spoons, to keep up appearances. I am sure they saw through her ruse, but she was very pretty and seemed so defenceless they left her alone. After the war we unearthed the treasure but the rags turned out to have been a mistake: they had attracted and held the moisture from the soil and the copper and pewter were badly stained. It took days to clean everything with chalk and kerosene and no matter how hard we polished, we never quite succeeded in restoring the old lustre.

Within half a year food was rationed. At first the rations seemed adequate. My mother and I were both small and had never been big eaters so there was enough for the three of us. Certain things could be bought without ration coupons: a horrendous gluey potato cake, and a kind of pink-coloured pudding you could prepare by adding skim milk to a greyish powder. My mother wouldn't buy these things because money was short and the nutritional value was questionable. But Wil, who was in his teens and growing fast, was always hungry and bought them with whatever money he could make doing odd jobs, and occasionally he let me have a taste of these delicacies. This is not to say that my mother had no cravings, but they did not run to sweets. She was a master at making "spreads" for sandwiches or toast. I don't quite remember how she did it, but fried onions, salt, pepper, curry, cumin, and chopped parsley came into it. What held it together was cooked oats and it tasted fantastic. As the war progressed and luxuries such as salt and tea became scarce we learned the true value of commodities we had always taken for granted. If ever a shortage should threaten now, I'd buy a large supply of salt, soap, tea, and candles, for those were the things we never got used to doing without.

One lifesaver was the discovery of the municipal central kitchen where people of slender means could obtain a reasonably nourishing meal at a price determined by a means test. With my father at sea and navigating for the allied forces – which meant there could be no communication or transfer of funds between him and us – our means were slender enough and we received our meal tickets at nominal cost.

Getting the food each afternoon was Wil's task. It was no more than a half-hour's walk to the kitchen and back but it was a dull walk through a bleak part of town and children would jeer at him, saying we were on welfare. Later everyone who could possibly qualify got their meals from the central kitchen, so by the time it was my turn to fetch the daily food there was no longer any stigma attached.

The dinners from the central kitchen were not very interesting but they were nourishing to a point. They mostly consisted of mashed potatoes with one vegetable or another: sauerkraut, cabbage, carrots and onions, turnips, kale. Occasionally we found some small scraps of meat, but mostly the only frill was a ladle of watery gravy.

ANTI-JEWISH LAWS

If in time we got used to meagre and monotonous meals, we never got used to the new regulations: cafés and restaurants, libraries, swimming pools, theatres, and movie houses were required to display signs at the entrances: "No Jews Allowed." Jews were ordered to stay indoors from 6 pm to 8 am, long before there was a general curfew for the population, and they were not allowed to stay overnight anywhere but in their own place. They had to wear a yellow Star of David with the word "Jew" printed in mock-Hebrew characters in the centre. Jewish teachers and university professors were fired. Gentile professors had to sign a statement declaring that they were not Jews, and if they refused (thank God some did) they were considered *Judenfreundlich* and were fired themselves.

Other regulations applied to the population in general. Demonstrations of any kind were prohibited, and offenders, mostly students, were rounded up and imprisoned. Artists, writers, and musicians were required to join the *Kulturkammer* – a sort of union instituted by the Nazis – whose members had to comply with Nazi directives. Refusal resulted in blacklisting. And of course any activities subversive of the new regime were forbidden and the penalties were horrifying. At one point all high executives of the national railways were ousted from their homes on short notice and their homes burned to the ground because it was claimed that they had sabotaged the orderly transports of goods and people leaving the country. Another time resistance workers killed a German officer near a village not far from Amersfoort and the Germans responded by deporting all the adult males in that village to Germany and Poland, where they subsequently died. We came to expect these acts of terror, and later, when we had become thoroughly involved ourselves, we knew exactly where we stood.

### MY MOTHER'S ANGER GETS TO THE BOILING POINT

During the first years of the war my mother rented out the two upstairs rooms in our house to help make ends meet. At the time the yellow stars became mandatory, the two rooms were let to two Jewish women, Stella and Nurse Oppen. The stars – each person had to *buy* four of them – were printed on flimsy yellow material, probably rayon, and had to be cut out before sewing them onto coat or jacket lapels. Stella cut hers out roughly and pinned the branding mark onto her coat any which way, merely to comply with the regulation. But Nurse

Oppen folded back the edges of each star and hemmed and pressed them meticulously before sewing them onto her clothes with tiny pretty stitches.

It was then that my mother began to think how she could help fight the wrong she perceived, not just passively, by refusing to hand over her brass and pewter, but by actively sabotaging Hitler's plans for the world. For although we had no facts, the deportations had now begun, and no one imagined that the Nazis were planning a picnic.

Jews were not the only ones who were rounded up and sent to "work" in Germany and Poland: the deportations included Dutch military officers, priests, ministers, teachers, striking dock workers – in short, anyone who had openly expressed distaste for the new order. And of course all those who were caught in the act of subversion were picked up and either shot on the spot or held for questioning and seldom released. But the Jews were picked up *for no reason* and it was the flagrant injustice of this that infuriated my mother.

One day two SD officers came to our house and asked for Nurse Oppen. Mother told them that she was at work, and that she did not know where that was, and the officers left. But we never saw Nurse Oppen again and this decided the issue for my mother. Stella had left to join her relatives in the eastern part of the country so the two rooms were empty again, and mother's hands itched to go to work. Soon after that Wil brought home an older friend of a friend, Eli, who had no place to hide. When she met him at the door my mother took one look at him and said, "All right, son, come in." And that was how it began. Before the month was out our family had grown to seven and every bed was taken.

## BEARING WITNESS

Not far from our house the Nazis had built a *Polizeiliches Durchgangslager*, a first-stop detention camp where prisoners waited for their case to come up, or else simply warehoused until enough of them warranted a large transport to Germany. That much we knew. What we didn't know was that hundreds of prisoners were executed there. Their mass graves were discovered after the war. Every day we saw small groups of prisoners being marched by our house on their way to the camp on 1914 Avenue, or from the camp to the station for their trip eastward.

Once inside, the prisoners were given the usual striped prison uniforms and their heads were shaven. Teams of ten or twelve had to work on the construction of shooting ranges for soldiers to practise. One of these ranges was being built at the barracks near our school. Around this time – it must have been summer 1943 – the municipal school board had somehow managed to put their hands on a consignment of milk and Spanish oranges, which were distributed to grade school children. We had to eat the oranges and drink the milk right in the classroom, to prevent them from finding their way onto the black market. But the peels of the oranges we could keep and take home to our mothers, who used them in cooking or in making a concoction we honoured with the name of marmalade, prepared with starch and saccharin. We prized these peels for their flavour though of course there was no nourishment in them.

On our way from school we used to stop by the shooting range to watch the prisoners at work. I don't know why we did it, but we did it every day. We were curious, of course, and felt pity and also relief that it was them and not our brothers or fathers behind the barbed wire fence. And part of it also was the thrill of the forbidden, for we were not allowed to stand at the fence and talk with the prisoners. One of them pushed a folded note through the fence once when the guard's back was turned for a moment. He was caught at the fence and the guard pulled him away roughly, shaking his fist at us and then pointing his rifle, which sent us scurrying. But I had picked up the note, which turned out to be a message to the prisoner's mother to say he was still alive but hungry and to please send food. My mother forwarded the message and packed up two slices of bread for me to give to the prisoner, but the next day he was not there so I gave the bread to one of his fellow-victims. As soon as the other prisoners saw food passing through the fence, a swarm of them descended on me, hands held out, but the bread was gone and all I had in my pocket were the peels of my orange. I held them up and they yelled, "Toss it over, quick!" but when I threw the peels over the chain link fence they turned away angrily. They thought I had oranges, not peels. One thin boy picked up the peels and started to chew them but they were too bitter and he dropped them with a hopeless gesture.

## PRISONER TRANSPORT
(*Mother*)

This morning a dozen shaven students, almost children,
two hooded, barefoot friars, eight or nine haggard Jews
marched by our house. Six SS soldiers guarded
the ashen prisoners shackled two by two.

This has been going on for months. I don't know
what scares the children more – the horror outside
or my furious tears. I can't spare them the sight
of either.

And all these months four fugitives hide in the backroom.
The children don't ask why, why do I risk our lives?
There is no need – the SS soldiers answer.

Each time we watch more prisoners from our window
the children grab hold of me as I cry again in anger.
Each time we thank God
our Jews can't witness
the facts that we compel ourselves to see and see.

WIL LEAVES US

In the third year of the occupation the SS began to pick up teenage boys off the streets to do odd jobs, either at the barracks or in the camp on 1914 Avenue. It was important to get Wil out of harm's way and my mother was able to have him placed in a merchant marine officers' training school in the north of Holland – a miracle in more ways than one. The Nazis apparently thought it was a good idea to let the school continue to operate because their plans for the Third Reich also included a merchant marine, so they would need trained personnel to man their fleet, and their own boys were all in the army. Of course Wil and my mother were convinced that that would never happen, as indeed it didn't. My brother set off to Enkhuizen, where the school was located, and where very soon after he met his future wife Christien who, barely seventeen, was the salt of the earth, and that was the other part of the miracle.

From then on my mother and I were the only legitimate occupants of our house on the park and were alone with our hidden friends who, as Eli later wrote, held no title to their lives.

OUR NEW FAMILY

The way our house filled up was simple. After Eli moved in, food and rations began to arrive – out of the blue, it seemed to me. A girl with a Boy Scout scarf tied round her head, and a scar on her lip, brought them every week. She was a courier for the resistance movement who helped place and maintain fugitives, and she could see that we had space enough in our house to accommodate a few more people, if mother would do it. She would, so the next day Joe and Lena Shapiro arrived, and a few weeks later Naomi, whose parents and brothers had been deported, and who got away from Amsterdam in the nick of time. The resistance workers sometimes brought sustenance in kind: a gunny sack of potatoes, a large bag of brown beans, and once three glass jars of thick pea soup. But mostly we had to exist on what we could buy with our ration coupons, which was less and less with each passing month.

The courier with the Boy Scout scarf brought ration coupons for all our guests and one extra set for the men. The coupons were stolen from the government distribution office while the administrator looked the other way, and I quickly learned that some forms of stealing were all right. Our combined rations would suggest a family of seven, if we were to buy all our supplies in one store. Since everyone in the neighbourhood knew that just two people, a mother with her daughter, occupied the house on the park, #18, we had to be careful to shop in three different stores. You could never be sure which merchant might notice and pass on the word to the *Gestapo* or even merely gossip about it. It really meant we had to shop in twelve different stores: three grocery stores, three vegetable stores, three bakers, and three milk stores. Only the butcher was guaranteed to be "good," as he was active in the resistance himself, but unfortunately he had less and less to sell, so that our seven sets of coupons often bought us no more than some soup bones or half a pound of kidneys.

It was a strange life we led, complicated and time-consuming and tense, but it was never confusing. We knew exactly what we were doing and why.

## TEAM
(*Mother*)

The enemy brings me
shoulder to shoulder
with my youngest child.

Any night may be the one
when we can't hide
our friends fast enough
from raiding soldiers.
Dawn is a gift.

Their survival my cause
my clear-cut task.
The grocer Shapiro
his pale wife Lena
the orphan Naomi
and Eli, my friend
inspire the venture
refuel my energy.

But outside this family
my own child Maria
independent and free
coming in, going out
my little comrade
fellow hewer and drawer
she keeps the grave secret
of our backroom as I do.

She sees what I see.
There is no option.
We're a team of two
against the dark.

## KEEPING WARM

Though food was a problem, and we were almost always somewhat hungry, it was still possible to adapt by thinking of something else. But fuel was a different matter. Now and then we could buy some coke, but it burned fast and gave off so much heat all at once, that the stone lining of our little black stove burned through and the iron casing bulged and sagged in places. A little old smith had to come from time to time to rivet patches on the weak spots.

Most of the time we had to buy wood on the black market from a man who cheated us on the weight. Once he brought us a particularly small load of what he said was a hundred kilograms of unsplit green pine logs, but as we had to have fuel to cook and heat the one room where we all lived, my mother reluctantly paid the exorbitant bill. Joe had watched from behind the curtain while the wood was unloaded and he told her: "I'll bet that he delivered no more than fifty kilograms." At dinnertime we went to the vegetable store and borrowed the owner's potato scales, and together we weighed the wood. Joe was right – he man had left just under fifty kilograms.

We returned the scales and stopped by the fuel merchant's to order another load of pine. When he delivered the load the next day, mother had him pile it neatly in the woodshed. When he was done she locked the door of the shed, put the key in her pocket, and thanked him kindly. When he asked for his money mother replied sweetly that she already paid him the day before, and fixed him with a level stare. When he understood what she meant he began to make a fuss, but then my mother ceased to be affable and played the outraged victim, turning on him with the threat that she would report him for black marketing. He did not stay long to argue the point, but after that we had to look elsewhere for wood.

## WOODS OPERATIONS I

A team of two workers sets out
earlier than possible
saw and hatchet
wheelbarrow oiled to ease
breaking and entering
the woods south of town.

Catching thieves – the warden tries not to –
his own home cold, but two a day
are a must. Today it is our turn.

Defeated we pass by the prisoner camp
on 1914 Avenue.
Across the road, opposite the gate
a half-cut birch, abandoned
crashed during the night.

We start hacking the windfall
under the SS guard's nose.
He looks away. Women and children
are not his department
unless they wear stars.

But an officer catches us
in the attempt – yells a tirade
about how he loved that tree
sat under it and dreamed
of home, and how could we …
tears in his eyes.

For the first time this war
I hear my mother in German:
look! I didn't cut this tree
I am just taking it home.
It's your fault!
Look at my child
skin over bones and no fuel …
tears in her eyes.

All right, go ahead then.
We work like horses till dark
taking turns sawing and wheeling
the loot home piecemeal.
The last load we take home together,
saw and hatchet on top of the wood.

I look at her sideways, she grins.
*My mother.* When it comes
to crocodiles she can hold
her own with Hitler's finest.

A DISCOVERY

I don't exactly remember when I first noticed that mother and Eli were more than just hostess and guest. We were all roommates of course, living together in the one room at the back, and separating only at night when the fire in the stove was quenched and we all went to our separate cold beds. We had no choice but observe one another, crammed together like that, and I suppose something in the way Eli and mother looked at each other had prepared me already for the conscious discovery I made one night.

I still used to come to my mother's room once in a while when I had had a bad dream and she would let me crawl in behind her in the big bed and sleep, spoon-fashion, till morning. It was on one of these occasions that I found there was no room for me. If I hadn't liked Eli so much – hadn't already cast him, perhaps from hunger, in the role of father, I would have been much more jealous than I actually was. Perhaps I knew in any case that I was too big to turn to my mother for protection from nightmares, but it was difficult to accept that now I had to go it alone. Young as I was, I had already begun to understand some of the less obvious facets of falling in love, such as the search for safety.

## CLEAR NIGHTS

A clear night in those days
always meant bombing
or the threat of it.
Outside – dark, and the whine
of high-flying bombers, the bark
of far-away flak.
Inside – in the room next to mine
my mother and Eli talking softly,
the bed sighing and laughing.

I knew what it was – they were lovers
but my hands
flat against the wall
knew nothing yet, felt only
that cold wall, barrier
between woman and child.

Then outside the barking again.
Hugging my warm empty space
blankets over my head
I shut out all threats
abdicated the world and thought
ah, Jesus, how you smile at me
from the picture in the children's Bible,
"suffer the little children"
though I was not so little
and took up all the room in his arms
no space for anyone else.

On those frightening nights
Eli and my mother
Jesus and I
found ways to endure a war.

## KEEPING BUSY

Eli and Joe had a hard time together. They had very different backgrounds and personalities: Eli the thinker and Joe the doer. It was difficult for them to find ways to pass the time. Eli was a good manager and helped my mother organise the household routines. Since mother and I were out a lot in the daytime on our foraging expeditions, most of the household tasks fell to our friends. Lena and Naomi prepared what food there was as attractively as possible and the men helped peel potatoes or apples or turnips. They would compete to see who could peel thinner, weighing the peels of one pound of potatoes. But Eli kept track of our supplies, dividing our weekly rations in daily portions, and arranging them neatly on shelves in our kitchen cupboard. The cupboard was small but the rations were smaller and there was plenty of space. He also wrote out lists of what we had, what we were likely to get, and what had been used up. He wrote letters and diaries as well, and worked out carefully what he was thinking at the time. But for that he had to be by himself and would sit in the bedroom until the cold drove him back to the others by the stove.

Through one of our resistance friends Joe had found work he could do for a man who owned a small button factory. At this plant they made buttons by cutting branches of beech trees in small discs, drilling holes in them, and then varnishing them, bark and all. Joe would receive these blank buttons and for hours every day he would sit by the window at the only table in the room and decorate each button painstakingly with tiny red and blue flowers and green leaves, with very small brushes.

By the standards of those times I suppose the buttons were not unattractive but as far as mother and I were concerned, the smell of the paint and the loss of the use of the table caused an enduring dislike for artsy buttons. There was more to it, though: I had to pick up the blank buttons from the manufacturer's house once a week and deliver the painted ones. The tires on my bike had long since worn out, and Eli and Joe had stretched lengths of old rubber garden hose onto the rims of the wheels, with the ends wired together. The button manufacturer lived near Soesterberg, where there was a military airbase which was regularly bombed while the highway traffic was also a prime target for RAF strafing.

The garden-hose tires made such a racket I could never hear the approach of the airplanes and had to stop now and then with my ear in the wind to find out if it was time to dive into one of the manholes dug along the road for the drivers of military transports. The treeless stretches of road – stretches which grew with every passing week thanks to our own attacks on any standing timber – were particularly nerve-wracking. The attacks were likeliest on clear days and I used to postpone my trips to the button man until the sky was overcast. Whether it was due to these precautions or to sheer luck I don't know, but I was never caught in an air raid, though that did not mean that my fear of bombing and shelling ever grew less. The dislike I sometimes felt for poor Joe had probably much less to do with his personality than with my own fear of being killed.

But that is what I say now. At the time I hated to be in Joe's presence for long. He was a kind and decent enough man, but we didn't look at the world the same way, didn't react to stress the same way. After months and months at close quarters with him, even the way he picked up his fork became a major irritation, and I am afraid I was too young to control my feelings and pulled faces more than once.

Still, mother and I were away in pursuit of the means of living a lot of the time. It must have been infinitely more difficult for Eli and Naomi and Lena, and for Joe himself, all forced together at such close range, and no escape.

Though I don't know the details, there were squabbles between them – no doubt about the defence of territory. I guess the territory in a sense included my mother and myself, to whom Eli had access on a quite different and much more relaxed level than Joe and Lena and Naomi did. While it gave him an edge in the pecking order, at the same time it laid him open to criticism for collusion with the enemy. For I have no illusions but that to Joe my mother and I must have represented the enemy in God knows how many ways. Granted, we were not Nazis, and were manifestly not after his life. But in a sense we were his jailers where he was our prisoner, we were free where he was confined to the house, we belonged where he was on sufferance, we were magnanimous where he had no choice but to be grateful.

Still, we were all in it together. Joe's life was in our hands, even in the hands of the impertinent little brat I was, whose secrecy he could hope for but not bank on. And yet our lives were also in his hands: one careless move, a curtain drawn back, a laugh laughed too loudly, an argument shouted too wildly, a light lit when mother and I were not home, any of these could have killed us all.

### HIDING PLACES

But Eli and Joe did find things to do together. They took precautions against their own death and against ours as well. They began building hideouts, starting in the attic where a small bedroom had been partitioned off with wood panelling, leaving a triangular tunnel between the partition and the sloping roof. Eli and Joe made an invisible hatch in the panelling, which could be fastened with latches on the inside, leaving no trace on the room side once the fugitives were behind the partitioning. All four of our guests slept in this crawlspace whenever raids threatened, but it was cramped and uncomfortable and above all, the location was obvious, even though the entrance panel was well-concealed. In a serious raid the searching soldiers would simply axe through the panelling or empty their guns through it, to make sure.

So in a next attempt at creating a safe space, they erected a partition in a large closet under the attic staircase. They used bricks to build the partition, and plastered it on the closet side. A hatch door sawn out of the stairs reached the space between partition and stairs. This was its weak point: when you mounted the stairs, the cut-out section always gave a little and squeaked, no matter how firmly they tried to support it from the inside. Moreover, the saw had left scars that would not be erased, no matter how carefully the two men blended Joe's button paints to match the green paint of the attic stairs.

The last and final hideout was made under the house. Like most houses in Holland, ours was built on a stone foundation on which beams supported a wooden floor. Underneath the beams was nothing but earth, and the space was kept fresh by four small screened air vents in the foundation at the front and back of the house. A trapdoor was made by sawing out the entire bottom of one of the cupboards in the living room, and next the men dug a deep and wide trench which they lined with bits of old carpeting and a tarpaulin we had in the attic.

Towards the end of the war the Germans were primarily interested in finding able-bodied men, and so our neighbour sometimes came to spend the night underground as well when rumours of new roundups had reached us.

## PRECAUTIONS AGAINST DEATH
(*Eli*)

By candlelight Shapiro and I
chip and scrape at the aged earth
under the house – a trench opens wide
to sleep four of us uneasily.

We spend days there and nights. When raids are on
the gentle woman who owns the house
lowers the trapdoor, answers the soldiers
while her child covers us with papers
then apples in rows: winter storage they'll say.

In hiding with us our give-away belongings
tell-tale photographs, signed letters
a menorah one of us saved. Shapiro nails
a tarnished mezuzah to the makeshift trapdoor –
Shaddai, the One Who said "Enough!"[1]
fails again to notice the irony.

## A FEAST

Lena was a wonderful cook. Once we had a goose brought to us by the little courier with the Boy Scout scarf, and my mother had managed to get a bag of hard sour cooking pears at the vegetable store, as well as some onions. First Lena simmered the goose on the back of the stove for a long time with nothing but water and a little salt. Overnight the stock cooled and in the morning Lena scooped off the fat, which was quite considerable. Then, with the onions and some potatoes and the stock, she made the most wonderful stew I ever had. But that was not all. She had Joe and Eli grind a few cupfuls of wheat in the hand-turned coffee mill and with that and the goose fat she made a thick, heavy dough. In the meantime Naomi had peeled the pears and quartered them, and they were simmering on the stove where the goose had cooked the previous day. Lena placed the dough on top of the simmering pears and pricked holes in it here and there so the pear juice could bubble up through the dough. Towards evening the cobbler, which Lena called pear*kugel,* was done and we could taste what had enticed us all day by its wonderful smell. In my entire life I have never tasted anything as perfect as Lena's *kugel,* nor have I ever tried to imitate it later. Its memory is sacred.

## I LEARN A TRADE TO LAST A LIFETIME

Lena was also an accomplished knitter. She and Joe had a little daughter who was in hiding with an unmarried schoolteacher in a nearby town. They had some contact with the child through the underground courier who would, on very rare occasions, bring the little girl on the back of her bicycle to visit with her parents for a few hours. One of the few things Lena could do for her child was knit, and knit she did. Little frilly dresses with matching bloomers and socks blossomed in her hands and cascaded in her lap. She knitted underwear and hats and scarves and mittens until there wasn't a scrap of yarn left in the house. She also taught me to knit socks and sweaters and together we unravelled my outgrown things and concocted two- and three-tone creations I thought were stunning and which certainly kept me warm for a time.

THE BABY THAT COULD NOT BE

Lena was a quiet, gentle woman and a master at smoothing her husband's often-ruffled feathers. They were very close and even though Lena was quite aware of Joe's rough edges, she never reproached him in our presence and always stood by him in any argument. In this house full of strangers, separated from his child, condemned to boring labour, always hungry and always afraid, Joe had one resource: Lena. He clung to her literally for dear life.

## SEPARATION

Joe Shapiro and Lena, Lena-and-Joe, married
fork against spoon in the narrow bed
a unit of two, until one grey morning
our doctor with his satchel goes upstairs in silence.
The rest of us wait in the cold blue kitchen.
It is raining softly. Nobody speaks.

Lena wan and alone in the narrow bed
while Joe on the couch, silent and helpless
waits for his woman to rise again, gingerly
holding her belly with both pale hands.

She now walks with dignity, aloof and quiet
mother of nothing. Joe's merely her husband
the separate father of a springtime yearning.
Lena has slept with this winter's darkness
the sire of her blank defeat.

## NAOMI FIGHTS HER OWN WAR

Naomi, the youngest of our friends and the last to join the tribe, was six or seven years older than I was, and when she came, her long glossy hair was a warm brown. She had a woman's full figure with large round breasts that in my eyes made her look like a goddess. My own chest was still "as flat as an ironing board with two peas" as my brother Wil put it derisively, but I had just begun to wake up to the riches that might be in store for me, too, and I admired Naomi immensely for her accomplishment.

She had an indomitable spirit and a playful nature, and tackled the drabbest tasks with a sense of adventure that carried her right through the grimmest winter. Since then I have always cherished the notion that big-breasted women are winners, and fun to be with.

## NAOMI

Mother says Naomi
wants to be someone
do something.
They took away her parents
her brothers
she's eighteen
she's stuck here.
Now someone has told her
all Jews have dark hair.
She's going to change that
tomorrow
with peroxide.
Please say nothing.

In the morning the sun shines.
I watch Naomi gently bleaching
Lena's black curly hair
parted neatly in strands.
Then she washes and combs it.
As it dries it turns chestnut.
Lena peers in the mirror
embarrassed and giggling
but Joe says it's all right.
I say nothing – it's lovely.

Then Naomi treats her own hair.
This time she is reckless
waits longer before rinsing.
When she's done it is carrots.

They laugh and debate
should she go one step further?
She picks up the comb
and repeats the process.
Now her hair feels like sisal
pale and lifeless.
I say nothing – this is how
Naomi charges history
head-on
with peroxide.

## I NEED A FATHER OR SOMETHING

Eli's place in our lives is not so easily described. Wil and I had had a pretty good relationship with our father before the war, but we were very young then, and when he came home there had often been a holiday atmosphere in the house. There would be the excitement of the reunion, noise and presents, and the glitter of uniforms. Then after a few days our dad would roll up his sleeves and get cracking on the many things that needed doing around the house. There would be the sound of sawing and hammering and the smell of freshly cut wood and varnish.

But later, by the time the marriage broke down, there would also be the sound of arguments behind closed doors, and our mother's soft crying, and we began to associate her red eyes and drawn face with my father's homecoming. It may have been different for Wil who probably needed a man to stand by him in that women's household, but speaking for myself, though I kept good memories of him, I did not really miss my father very much when he was gone. Still, I did need a man in the family for safety.

My mother's brother Jan was the one I picked. Or perhaps he picked me, for when I was a baby, during the Depression, he had been out of work for a time and had helped my mother nurse me through a serious attack of the whooping cough. Ever since that time it was he, rather than my almost always absent father, on whom I pinned my expectations of male warmth and affection, and I loved it when he visited. When I returned home from school and saw his bike leaning against the side of the house, I would sprint the last few hundred yards to see him sooner. He came often, after my parents' separation, both to give comfort and to receive it, I suspect, since his own life was not very smooth at that time either, and my mother was his best friend. Once, when he was there at the table, having tea, there was no extra cup for me on the tray when I came home, and mother told me to get a clean one from the cupboard, but I said no, I could use Jan's. "That's what I call real love!" he laughed, and I guess he was right.

But as the occupation dragged on, it became harder and harder to keep in touch. Jan lived no more than an hour's bike ride away from us, but as our bicycles wore down and no new tires could be had, the 15-km distance became an insurmountable obstacle and we saw less and less of him. When pleasure travel by train was prohibited altogether in the last year of the war we stopped seeing each other entirely.

This did not mean I stopped loving him, of course, and the Jesus of my lonely nights resembled nobody as much as Jan, but he wasn't there to talk with and touch, and Eli was. My relations with Eli were quite different. He was old enough to serve as a surrogate father, and there wasn't very much I could not discuss with him if I felt like it, for I trusted him without reservation. But he was also young enough to rumble with, as with a big brother. We used to play wild silly games, playing tag in the house: out the living room door, into the hall, then into the dining room and from there into the living room again, round and round in a circle. If you were it, you could change directions when you were out of sight, and scare the other one out of his wits when he suddenly ran into you. Wil and mother had invented that game and used to play it until they were both faint with laughter. Eli learned fast, and when Wil left for his naval training, I played it with him. Or he'd pick me up and toss me high up in the air and catch me again, for I was a sliver of a girl, a little "snippet" as he used to call me. So when I realised that he had become my mother's lover I didn't mind. He would do as a stepfather.

## MY MOTHER DISREGARDS THE COMMANDMENTS

We had some strange traditions in our family. My mother used to go out sometimes, just before sundown, without saying where exactly she was going. She just "went for a walk," with a pair of garden clippers in her pocket. Half an hour later she'd be back with her loot. She had done nothing less than poach: half a dozen sprays of forsythia or lilac, a little bunch of lily-of-the-valley, some flowering crab, or pussy willow, or a branch or two of colourful leaves or berries – whatever was in season. Usually she confined her raids to the public parks, but if any creeping plant ventured on the street side of a fence she'd consider that fair game too.

Eli was not brought up with such a nonchalant attitude to the Ten Commandments and always shook his head, half in reproach and half in admiration, when my mother came home with another armful of evidence of her small-scale lawlessness. But whatever he thought, we always had something green or flowering in the room, no matter how poor we were or how bleak the times.

## BURNT BUTTERCUPS

A Jew hides from Nazis
in my mother's house
I love him as only
small girls can love
grown men

He hides and hides
For three whole years
no sunlight
no windblow
no raindrench

One day I pick buttercups
on my way from school
their hearts bringing home
aching memories of butter

In the hallway he pounces
like a mad dog, snarling
ripping the flowers
from my hands, crushing
before the fire wilts them,
melts them

He gives me a reason
for his fury –
I destroyed nature
shortened their lives
for my pleasure
But he does not fool me

## SHOPPING FORMS A BOND

My mother and I talked a lot while we were foraging for food and fuel or for books for Joe and Lena. We almost always talked of what we were doing: which grocer was nicer, Terpstra, or Verhagen, or Beel; or the way Beel's daughter pronounced the word "jam" to come out something like "schem" and thought she knew better than anyone. Things like that. Or we would discuss the relative virtues of oak over pine. Oak was harder to cut and saw, while you could cut down a pine and saw it and get away in an hour. But while it took longer to get a load of oak ready for the stove, it lasted longer, too, so you didn't need as much. But pine smelled nicer and there was more of it in the woods. And so on.

But when we went to get books mother really came into her own. She was an avid reader, or used to be when there was time, and she read German, French, and English literature with ease, or did, before the war. Now German was out. Even her beloved Mann was tainted since she could not rid herself of associations, hearing and hating his language now that we heard our oppressors snarl it all around us. And English was out, too, since bookstores could no longer sell anything in that language, and the public library had had to take English books off the shelves.

Mother was something of a literary snob and did not think Dutch novelists amounted to much, though she didn't mind the poets. But then again, poetry in those days was not what it is now, it was not *engagé*. Most of it had to do with loneliness, and nature, and death – that sort of thing. But who would read about the "whispering leaves in the spring-time woods" when the idea of "tree" meant protection on the road from strafing, or heat in the stove? Who felt lonely when there wasn't even a moment to be alone? And about death you wouldn't need to *read* exactly.

Katherine Mansfield had been one of my mother's favourite writers, and Virginia Woolf had been one, and D.H. Lawrence. She told me some of the stories in their books – I had no English and would have been too young in any case to read the books myself – and her enthusiasm made me aware of these writers so that when the time came I was ready for them.

In the meantime we got romances for Joe and Lena from the little lending library on the main street where, mother said, they didn't have a single book she'd want to read. She didn't say so at home – only to me, in confidence, and I felt proud and privileged to be her confidante, and kept this secret carefully from Joe and Lena, not to spoil their pleasure. I felt so responsible: being trusted with this relatively trivial insight into the workings of my mother's mind seemed much more tangible than the other, official secret I had to keep, as if our happiness was more important than our lives.

### WHAT MAKES TWO PEOPLE HAPPY?

She may not have read romances, but my mother was an accomplished romantic all right. Even her marriage to my father at a very young age had begun with a wild infatuation and lasted as long as it had because she had had such high hopes for the four of us and believed you could make marriage work if you worked at it hard. In addition, she was stubborn and hated to give up. God knows what makes a marriage happy. I certainly did not, at that time or ever, but I did know that my mother loved Eli, and he her. The search for safety and the need for spiritual support under wartime stress may very well have been part of the process that made them turn to each other, but the warm feeling between them had nothing to do with all that. It was simply there, and it saw them through the war and well beyond.

I have an image of them engraved on my memory. It was in our cold blue kitchen, where either mother or Lena did the cooking until the gas supply was cut off. My mother stood stirring something in a pot on the stove, and Eli stood behind her with his arms around her and his chin resting lightly on the top of her head. They were just standing there, saying nothing.

SONG OF SONGS
(*Mother*)

I am in love
Is there news in such a thing?
I slept alone for years
and now my own son's friend
is my friend. What is new
in such a thing is that his voice
touches me now in such unguarded spots.

> His voice is
> altogether lovely
> this is my beloved
> and he is my friend

So I'm in love
The usual reasons why
I'm bred to feed and shield
so now my own son's friend
needs me. What's odd
in such a thing is that his face
touches me now beyond my own control.

> O my love
> in the dark of my house
> in the shadow of these walls
> let me see
> let me hear
> your voice
> your face

I did not wake
this love before it pleased
but you waited in the wings of my nights
and now, my own son's friend,
love me. What's right
in such a thing is that your hands
touch me now, shaping a solid shield
against the dark.

    Yes I have set you
    as a seal upon my heart
    for our love is strong as death

## THE WINDFALL

A few doors down from us, at #15, there lived an elderly couple, the Hansens, who were born German. They had lived there for many years, since long before the war, and never bothered anyone, but now they often had German officers visiting them and that really did bother us a lot. When we saw the officers go in with bags and parcels which we suspected contained things to eat, Mother and I fantasised about the parcels' contents and thought up all kinds of exotic things, like canned meat and sugar, tea and soap and cheese.

One day we had a chance to partake of this bounty in a curious way. Milizza, our cat – as thin as we were, but probably not quite as hungry, for there were always mice and sparrows – came home one day dragging a round thing. It seemed to be a disc the size and colour of a pancake but about five times as thick. She could barely move it and had to stop now and then, but slowly she advanced in the direction of the house. It was the cat's determination that alerted my mother: she went out to investigate and came back with the disc in her hands and Milizza at her heels. We inspected the find with care. It was slightly thicker in the middle than at the edges and heavy, and after we all had guessed for a while my mother suddenly realised what it was: cheese! It was a cheese, a small luncheon cheese that had once been a soft round ball, but had been left on a shelf and had spread and hardened into this indefinable object.

Immediately we thought, "Aha, Hansen!" since who else could afford to let a cheese sit on a shelf until it was no longer recognisable? And as if we had gained a private victory over the Germans it filled us with glee to keep this small quantity of food the Hansens probably didn't even miss or might even have discarded. My mother soaked it overnight in cool water and next day she scraped off the mouldy crust with the back of a knife until the orange-golden rind was exposed, smooth and firm and mouth-watering. With Wil's compasses she divided the circular cheese in six equal parts and gave us each a wedge while poor Milizza, who sang high and low for her cheese, had to make do with the rinds.

## A BAD SCARE

The hiding place under the house was used on several occasions. When SS soldiers searched houses, they usually went about it quite methodically and started at one end of the street to work their way down. As a result, there usually was enough warning and the fugitives could disappear down into their hiding place, while my mother and I spread newspapers and apples or cooking pears or onions or whatever we happened to have on the trapdoor, and tidied away any possible clues. Any thorough search by military personnel who had been tipped off would no doubt have revealed the flaws in the charade we offered, but routine searches usually went no further than a fast trip through the house by the soldiers, and a cursory look in every room and closet.

But once we were unlucky. We were all upstairs in the room at the back when there was a knock on the door and my mother went down to see who it was. It was just before the evening curfew and she expected to see the courier to bring the news, but instead there were two German officers. They asked if there were any men in the house and my mother said no, there weren't. One of the officers, looking incredulous, said to his companion, *Glaubst du das, sie sagt sie hat keinen Mann!* Mother was quick to perceive their scepticism as a compliment and played the part. Smiling demurely she said, "No, really, my husband is at sea (without mentioning that he sailed for the allied forces) and my son is at officers' training school in Enkhuizen." Then she called over her shoulder, "Oh, Maria!" and I came down innocently to corroborate her story, though I didn't even know what it was.

The officers checked their list and nodded, evidently finding that this information tallied with what the neighbours on the left had told them about us. Then they asked mother who the people next door on the other side were, what they did for a living, how many people there were in the house, etc. Mother said politely that she didn't know exactly, that she had fallen out with the neighbours years ago, but that she thought there was an old lady with two grown daughters. (In reality we knew the neighbours quite well – one of the daughters was married and the other engaged, and they all worked in the resistance movement.)

The officers left, and it took us the rest of the evening to recover from the fright, but the next morning a young subaltern came to the door before we were even up and about. He sounded crisp and businesslike and told my mother he had been informed that she had a room to spare, and he had orders to billet two privates on us. Would my mother please show him the room they could use. Mother calmly asked him to step inside and told him to wait downstairs while she woke up her daughter who slept in that room. She went upstairs without haste, woke up Eli who really slept there with her, and sent him to the room at the back where Lena and Joe were still unaware of what was going on. Then she went to my small room and told me to put on a bathrobe and sit on the edge of the big bed and pretend that it was mine. When the subaltern came in, I sat rubbing my eyes and he withdrew hastily, saying fine, that room would do, but did she have a place for me? My mother said oh yes, I could sleep with her, or else in the attic.

The billeted soldiers came in the afternoon. Mother had stripped down the bed, taken the mattress off the box spring, and cleared the room of anything that had made it pleasant before. Not a book, not a plant, not a rug remained and the soldiers were left to fend for themselves. They looked incredibly young, even to me, and their faces were as grey as their uniforms, as if they were cold through and through. There was a small heating stove in the room and they made a fire with coal they brought themselves from the barracks. They also had their own blankets, and they used their clothes for pillows. From dawn to dusk they were gone to the training grounds, and the only favour they asked was hot water for shaving, first thing in the morning.

They stayed for three weeks, and I'll never know how we managed to carry on, with six people in the house instead of the two who officially lived there. We crept about up and down the stairs, washed, cooked, used the toilet, and all this right under the nose of these two fledgling enemies. To tell the truth, I think the two boys in the front bedroom couldn't care less. They came, dropped down on their bed and slept, shaved, and left, every day for three weeks. On the day they finally left for the front they came down to the kitchen and asked me, *Wo ist die Mutti?* I told them she was out and they muttered that that was too bad, they had wanted to thank her for being so kind to them. And I think that was one time when my mother felt some real remorse for holding so dogmatically to her resolve not to aid or abet the enemy. They had tidied their room to a tee, cigarette butts in the lid of a jam jar, newspapers folded, and they had left us the rest of their coal, two tins of beans, and a bar of soap.

## THE WALLS HAVE EARS

We were all excellent at keeping secrets. Even my next-door girlfriend Marion's parents, whose kitchen window faced ours, did not know for sure that four people were hiding with us for three years, though later they told us they had suspected it: they were close enough to hear the toilet being flushed remarkably often. We didn't talk about our guests with anyone. My friendship with Marion suffered a bit, for she could no longer come to our house and we had to play either outside or else in her house. The apparent one-sidedness of our friendship irritated her mother, and though after the war it was all explained and "forgiven," Marion and I had by then grown apart and had found new friends.

But for a long time we held onto each other against all odds. Playing outside till curfew had its own attractions. The park on which we lived had two ponds, one slightly higher than the other, and between the two ponds were two small cascades connecting the higher to the lower pond. In between the cascades was a little island, with ornamental shrubs and a pepper tree, which flowered in spring with mysterious purple flowers. Marion and I considered this island our home away from home, and we had our "serious conversations" there. The existence or non-existence of God was a favourite topic. We discussed this with the same interest as we discussed the virtues of Marion's seventeen-year-old cousin Linda whom we both admired for her blue eyes and blond hair, or the excellent qualities of my uncle Jan, whose existence by this time had almost become an article of faith.

## MORE LAW-BREAKING

Added excitement to our outdoor existence was provided by the park superintendent, who had two jobs. One was to supervise work crews cutting grass and pruning trees, and the other was to keep children off the grass and out of the trees. Judging by the energy and hours he spent on it, this second job must have been by far the more satisfying to him and his zeal made the island a much more interesting place for us than it would otherwise have been. We kept a sharp eye out for him, and when we saw him coming on his bike, we would duck behind the shrubs. As he slowly circled the twin ponds to inspect his territory from the gravel path, we kept circling at the same rate, always keeping out of his sight. Sometimes this worked, and we got away with it. At other times we were caught and reprimanded. Once he took us home to our mothers, and when he came to our door with me and delivered his little speech he added, "After all, we want to bring up our daughters to be little ladies, don't we?" My mother cocked her head and said slowly, "Well, no, not particularly – " and when, taken aback, he rode off on his bike shaking his head, mother and I fell into each other's arms, faint with laughter. As with her theft of forsythia at dusk, here, too, my mother's regard for the law depended on circumstance.

## MORE WINDFALLS

Our outdoor activities, combined with ever-present hunger, sharpened our hunting instincts as well. In early October the beeches dropped their nuts and we would go to the main street to gather them. Not all trees bore nuts. Some had nuts that were empty, so they were no good. Some years were good and others poor, but the fall of 1944 delivered a bumper crop. Heavy military traffic during the night left a thick blanket of crushed nuts on the road so in the morning we could see at a glance which trees were yielding. We squatted on the sidewalk with our tins amid dozens of other children, and gathered all morning and again all afternoon.

The beechnuts were reddish-brown and shiny: tiny triangular nuts growing two by two in a rough little husk. It was easy to tell if a nut was hollow: it collapsed when you squeezed it hard between your finger and thumb. But we were old hands at this job and didn't need such a sledgehammer approach. We could tell by the slight swelling of the flat sides at the base of the nut if it was full or empty, so we sorted as we gathered, taking no time even to eat any. Opening a beechnut with your nails was not so wonderful in any case, since the sharp tip of the nut caught under your nail and made it sore after a while.

At home came the rewards of sitting on your haunches all morning and afternoon. You got out the skillet and roasted the nuts on top of the stove. The tough brown skin would crack with a pop that made the shelling afterwards easy. Then came the moment of glory – pouring the nuts onto a newspaper in the middle of the table for all to gather around: half a cupful of nutmeats each.

## A NEW SCHOOL AND A NEW FRIEND

In the fall of 1943 I went to junior high school and made a new friend for life. Her name was Eva. She was a year older than I was but she was shy and did not feel comfortable with her classmates. Her house was a short distance from mine and our friendship began with our walking home together. Eva's parents were elderly and Eva was mature for her age. She had read books I had never heard of and had an interesting, philosophical way of thinking that set her apart from other girls I knew. She was a very different sort of girl than Marion, who was nothing if not practical: one of the things she told me in our serious conversations on the island was that she wanted to marry a boy with curly hair so her children would have curls.

Eva fascinated me and I felt flattered that she, a year older and a grade ahead of me, would think it worth her while to have me for a friend. Perhaps her studious and serious nature was attracted to my childishness in kicking a particular pebble all the way home from school, or in wanting to play with her doll's house that was sitting neglected in a dark corner of her attic. It never occurred to me to ask. One thing that clearly caught her imagination was the secret of our hidden friends and the love affair that had blossomed between Eli and my mother, but I didn't tell her about that until much later, when the war was nearly over, and by that time our friendship was well-established.

Eva's parents were kind and hospitable and welcomed their daughter's friend to their home, so I would often come in with Eva after school and play for an hour before going home to do my chores. I was painfully thin then, so thin that it scared Eva's mother and once a week, on Sundays, I was asked to stay with them for supper. This meant that I could stay overnight as well since the early curfew would not let me go home after the meal. I can't actually remember feeling hungry, but I can recall those meals with such pinpoint clarity that I can only conclude I must have been starved. Eva's father was well to do and could afford to buy privately from the farmers, or on the black market, so the meals seemed opulent to me. Before the war the family had lived in what was then the Netherlands East Indies and their taste ran to spicy dishes that were new and exciting to me. In addition, they had salt and some sugar, which they used in the preparation of these sumptuous meals. Instead of rice they used barley, served with a thick sauce made of onions and garlic and hot chilli peppers. There was usually cabbage fried in oil with onions and curry, and for dessert there would be porridge made of oats or grits boiled in skim milk and sweetened with syrup. Those were festive meals indeed, served at the dining room table on lovely white Wedgwood plates with rims that resembled basketwork.

IN THE DARK

We hadn't had gas for cooking for quite some time, so people cooked on their heating stoves, but when in the fall of 1944 electricity was also cut off, the dark descended in earnest. Candles and kerosene were only available on the black market and we couldn't afford them. A poor substitute for an oil lamp was a "floater:" a cotton wick was threaded through a cork disc that floated on the surface of cooking oil in a small glass. These floaters gave off a little light but more sickening stench and in addition we saw our food go up in flames, so we were always looking for alternatives. One day my mother got hold of a pile of hardboard scraps through our connection with the button man, and Eli and Joe cut these up with a hand saw to make long narrow strips which we burned as torches at night. One of us would stand with the torch over the stove when there was cooking to be done or over the table when we had our meal or read or played a card game before going to bed. But this was a tiresome job – you felt like one of those boys with a fan behind Pharaoh's throne, keeping off the flies. One day Eli had a brainwave and attached a clip to the top of a tripod. The hardboard strip was then clipped to the tripod at an angle to minimise smoking, but it still smoked a lot and the charred curling end had to be knocked off and caught in a bin every few minutes. Still, the strips gave off a fair amount of light and allowed us to knit or read for half an hour before bedtime. Lena and I had become quite handy at knitting in the dark and produced many a sock, knitting away boredom. Even after all those years, I never lost the touch, and can still knit without looking at my work, while reading or watching television.

We also played a lot of games in the dark. Naomi was a crackerjack at games and introduced us to "proverbs." One of us would leave the room while the others thought of a particular proverb. Then the one on the landing was called back in and had to ask questions on any subject of each of the others in turn. The answer had to contain one word of the proverb in sequence, and the trick was to guess the proverb in the least number of questions. We would also play "broken telephone," but six people were not really enough for that. And we would tell stories, or invent stories by thinking up lines in turn, or make word chains of compound words, each one beginning with the last part of the previous one: wood work, work gear, gear shift, shift lock, lock smith, etc. But we ran out of proverbs and got bored with the other games and with each other's voices and predictable ways. Tempers wore thin in our little backroom. What we felt, I suppose, was a form of battle fatigue, and to prevent ourselves from biting each other's heads off, we would retire earlier and earlier, thinking that bed was probably as good a place as any when you weren't feeling all that marvellous.

Again, if my mother and I felt edgy, we could escape in the morning. But what about Joe and Eli, what about Naomi, and how did Lena feel? She and Joe slept in the room where the stove was, our communal living room. Day in day out she'd get up, make the bed, get the stove going, boil ground wheat or rye in water and serve it, one ladle per person, to the rest of the family. No doubt she felt she compared unfavourably with Mrs. Bumble. Day in day out she'd settle the stove after breakfast, feeding it small bits of wood to keep it going, but only just. Then dusted the furniture, washed the dishes, watered the geranium in the windowsill and sat down, day after day, to watch the rain on the windowpanes, to watch Joe paint his buttons, to watch the paint dry.

**WORN**
(*Lena*)

Third day it rains
this windowsill needs paint
I paint my nails blood red
something to do
Joe paints his flowers
oh God flowers in winter
such prettiness
on bits of nothing – vain
the stove will ruin my nails
it has to burn
to warm what's left of us.
This windowsill needs paint
the house needs paint
oh God my heart needs paint
it is so grey.

## BEGINNING TO FIND OUT THAT EVA WILL BE A FRIEND FOR LIFE

The schools were closed in the fall of 1944. There was no fuel to keep the classrooms heated, several teachers had been deported for their political leanings, and others had gone into hiding. The students were urged to take home their textbooks and study by themselves. Eli tried to help me with my algebra, but I was lazy and easily distracted, he was impatient and we were both testy, so we gave that up for a bad job.

The only cheer left at that time were my visits to Eva's. Her family was conventional in the best sense of the word: father, mother, sister and brother, living in a big house as comfortably as possible under the circumstances. In the afternoon the parents would sit by the fire and read, but both would look up from their books when Eva and I came in. Eva's mother poured the tea made of cherry stems, and listened to us talk about ourselves. Eva's father would give us his views on the news in *The Nutshell,* the stencilled newsletter put together by an underground organisation whose members had access to a short-wave radio receiver that picked up the BBC broadcasts. The bulletin always told us the exact opposite of what we read in the Nazis' posted bulletins. Eva's father, by his commentary, taught us to read critically, whether the information came from the right or from the left, and not to read the news as we wished it were.

I had to leave by five to make it home to do my chores, and when I went to say goodbye, Eva's mother would be in the kitchen preparing supper. No matter how simple their meal, the table in the dining room would be covered with a cloth and set carefully with the white Wedgwood plates they also used on Sundays when I stayed for supper. Perhaps it was the contrast with my own mother's cavalier attitude towards the virtues of order, peace, and moderation that attracted me so much to Eva's orderly home. In any case, my visits offered a temporary escape from our strange, tightly-packed heterogeneous household where the meals were served in bowls held on our knees, so that four of the six of us could disappear underground at the first sign of danger, leaving no trace.

Eva could never play at our house. Lena and Joe particularly were deathly afraid that their presence would be discovered. This fear was not imaginary – people who knew too much were time bombs: once caught and subjected to cross-questioning, they might divulge everything they knew and take dozens of resistance workers and their charges with them into the abyss. The less you knew, the better it was. You never asked questions, and you did not volunteer information, those were the rules we lived by. And you never brought your friends home to play.

SINGING CURES ALL

There was a retired clergyman in town, Dominee Noorda, who had a plain daughter in her thirties, Renée. There were whispered rumours that Renée had had a fiancé or lover who was in the resistance and who had been caught and executed right in front of her house. No one knew about this at first hand, though, and I, cruel in my youthful ignorance, had my doubts that Renée could ever have had a lover, she was so plain. But Renée knew two things: she knew how to sing and she knew how to teach. So it made sense that she taught singing in her father's church.

I can't recall how Marion and I got involved, since neither of us went to church, and even if we had gone, we wouldn't have attended Dominee Noorda's church. However, once a week we went to Renée's music classes. They began in October. With empty stomachs we'd walk the mile to the unfamiliar little church in rain or sleet and sing for all we were worth. For an hour and a half we forgot everything, carried along on the current of Renée's enthusiasm and strength. She had such presence, and was so kind to us, that we listened to her as we had listened to no other teacher before and her face became lovely in the course of time. Her excellent ear helped us develop an ear of our own, and though our voices were just what they were, unexceptional, she taught us how to use them to best advantage.

Most of the songs we sang were traditional Christmas carols, some quite old, and we learned to shape our mouths around the unfamiliar Latin of *In Dulce Jubilo* and *O Sanctissima* until they came as easily as any Dutch song of later date. The harmonisations she used were modern and made the songs sound exotic, and for a few hours each week we were not bothered by our hunger and we lost our fear of the Nazis and the bombings and listened in astonishment to the harmonies our own voices produced.

On Christmas Eve Renée organised a pageant. I don't remember what the plot was, or even if there was one. But I remember the songs we sang and the robes we wore, made of old sheets trimmed with tinsel our mothers kept in the attic from Christmases past. And whether from weakness or emotion, our audience was in tears.

## THE FORAGING COUNCIL

After Christmas that year we really didn't have a single thing left to eat in the storage cupboard. By this time all that the ration coupons entitled us to was half a loaf of unspeakable bread a week per person, made of potato peels and bran, one half pint of cooking oil per person a month, and the daily soup from the central kitchen consisting of turnip, potato peels, and water. You could not live on this, but there was nothing else. Joe began to have fainting spells and had to spend a lot of time in bed, both to conserve what strength he still had, and to keep from falling. Eli was smaller and wirier and seemed a little better able to keep going, though not much better. It was all he and Naomi could do to keep enough wood cut for the stove.

We held a family council and it was decided that mother, together with Lena – her hair freshly touched up by Naomi – would go to the eastern part of the country to barter with the farmers. Aside from the strafing on the open road, this was not too dangerous for my mother, since she would not be alone: thousands of city women and children undertook similar foraging expeditions, called *hunger trips,* for their families. But for Lena it was dangerous. A child could tell that her hair was not naturally red, and her falsified identity card – from which the J for Jew had been erased, and on which her real name Shapiro had been changed to the more neutral Dutch name of Scholten – would not have stood up under anything but the most cursory examination. Still, she was the better candidate, since Naomi's card was even more poorly doctored than Lena's, and she was considered to "look more Jewish," whatever that meant.

Joe was flat against this plan, but the others, including Lena herself, with her usual *sangfroid,* overrode his protests. There was no choice really, since mother could not go alone and I was too short and too slight to handle a heavily laden bike. And who knows but Lena might have come to the point where anything seemed better than staying at home.

These hunger trips were usually made on bikes with saddle-bags, or with little carts made of crates on bicycle wheels, or with prams, or kiddiecarts – anything that would roll. Joe and Eli did the best they could with the two remaining bikes. They fitted them with new garden-hose tires, oiled the wheels and the pedals, and above all they tightened all the nuts and bolts that held the luggage carriers in place, since they would have to carry all that the women could gather.

## SMOKE OF THE MORNING
(*Joe*)

I hate this room, cold mornings, the smell of my own breath
but I can stand it if you're with me, Lena.
This nothing-food, these pre-war books, my silly work
nothing means anything when you're not here. I want
the sun, Lena, the rain to soak me but we have the smoke
the darkness of cold mornings, even in bed
when we are warm I can't quite have you, Lena.
She wants to take you with her. She and that girl
and Eli, even you yourself decided it is better so
but not for me it isn't – what if I faint again
Lena, what if I

Lucie and Jaap engaged, 1925

Jaap, 1930

Lucie, 1930

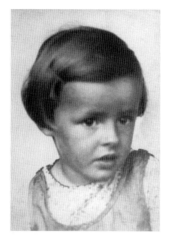
Maria, 1933

Wil, 1942

Wil and Maria on the sled their father Jaap made, 1933

Eva Zomer, 1942

Maria still looking a little underfed, 1945

Wil and Christien, 1944

Wil, 1946

The "safe house" in Amersfoort, 1945   Another angle of the "safe house" in Amersfoort, 1945

Eli, 1947

Naomi with bleached hair, 1944

Naomi with her natural hair colour again, 1946

Naomi in Palestine, 1946

Naomi on the job in Belgium in her boiler suit. On the back of the photo Naomi has written, "The girl who'll never forget you." Nov. 28, 1945

Maria gaining weight, 1946

Maria's passport photo, 1951

Maria sailing in the north of Holland, 1947

Lucie, 1947

Wil and Christien at City Hall on their wedding day, 1948

My uncle Jan in mid life

Lucie was visiting us in Canada at Christmas. We celebrated it with my aunt in the U.S. and Eli surprised us all by turning up unannounced, 1974.

The tree planting at the Avenue of the Righteous Gentiles in Jerusalem, 1983

Wil, Lucie, Naomi, and Maria at the tree-planting ceremony in Jerusalem, 1983

The ceremony at Yad Vashem in Jerusalem, 1983

# DIPLÔME D'HONNEUR

Le présent Diplôme atteste qu'en sa séance du 26 Octobre 1982 la Commission d'Hommage aux Justes des Nations, établie par l'Institut Commemoratif des Martyrs et des Héros Yad Vashem, sur la foi des témoignages recueillis par elle, a rendu hommage à **Wilhelmina L.M.J. Wolsak-Mendelson; Marja et Wilhelm** qui, au péril de leur vie ont sauvé des Juifs persécutés pendant la période de l'Holocauste en Europe, leur a décerné la Médaille des Justes parmi les Nations et les a autorisés à planter un arbre en leur nom dans l'Allée des Justes sur le Mont du Souvenir à Jérusalem.

Fait à Jérusalem, Israël, le
18 Octobre 1983

The certificate presented to Lucie, Maria, and Wil at Yad Vashem in Jerusalem, 1983

Maria at the time the first edition of this book was published in 1983.
Photograph by Reg Innell/Toronto Star

## A TERRIFYING RESCUE

One more raid had to be made on the wood stand halfway up the hill near our house, to lay in enough fuel to last us during the women's absence. It had snowed, and it was a good time to use the sled my father had made for us, years before, when I was still a little thing. A photograph of the time when the sled was just finished shows Wil and me sitting on it, cheek to cheek, Wil in a dark tracksuit and I in a light fluffy coat. We looked like the ideal brother-sister pair, chubby and healthy and affectionate and well off. Of all these properties only my father's sled remained, and it came in handier now than ever before.

Naomi, disappointed that she could not go on the hunger trip, convinced my mother to at least let her come to get the wood, while I stayed home to do her chores. Mother gave in, for she could see that Naomi was close to an attack of cabin fever and badly needed some fresh air. Her decision to let Naomi come also had something to do with the fact that the Germans, this late in the war, were so busy rounding up able-bodied men to work in the factories that they had little time to spare to fish for small fry, women, even if they were Jewish. Naomi was looking forward to bringing in the wood so much she could hardly sleep and was up at dawn. As soon as curfew allowed, the women set out so they might get a head start on the warden. Counting on the sled to do most of the work they quickly cut down six thin pines, took off their branches and lifted them whole onto the sled, tied them up and started for home. All the while Naomi kept sniffing and breathing in the frosty air as if it had to last her forever.

The downhill part gave them no problems but nearer home they hit a rough spot and got stuck in the middle of the dirt road. After a struggle with the loaded sled they were just about to untie the trees when they heard behind them the sound of hooves and a horse-drawn military transport wagon came into sight. There was nothing they could do to hide either themselves or the wood, so they pretended not to notice and kept on fussing with the sled. The horses stopped, the two soldiers jumped down from the seat and advanced upon them, and in their mind's eye the women saw their trees, saw, axe, and sled confiscated and carted away, themselves arrested ...

At this stage in the war all young German soldiers were at the battlefronts, if they weren't already dead, and the occupying troops left behind consisted mainly of elderly men. They were called the "kerosene men" because in their shabby, make-shift uniforms, they looked like the little old fellows with peaked caps who used to sell kerosene from door to door for lamps and cooking stoves in days gone by.

The two soldiers bearing down on my mother and Naomi were kerosene men. *Nun, was gibt's denn?* one of them asked amiably. In their nervousness mother and Naomi giggled – what did he think was going on, a game of marbles? The soldiers bent down and tried to pry the sled loose for the women, but got no further than they had, so they untied the ropes, heaved the trees into the empty cart, threw in the sled after them and without ceremony lifted Naomi and my mother in as well. Over his shoulder the driver asked my mother where she lived, and five minutes later wood, tools, sled, and women were unloaded at the curb in front of our house and the soldiers drove off, waving.

Eli and I, having been on the lookout behind the curtains in the upstairs front bedroom, nearly fainted when we saw the grey military cart stop at the curb but we stayed at the window, mesmerised. Lena and Joe in the back room were spared both the fright and the relief of that spectacle, but not the endless telling and retelling of the whole breathtaking story. Mother and I brought the trees to safety behind the house. Later, after dark, we would open the French doors and carry the trees inside. The men and Naomi would saw the logs right in the living room. The sawhorse had worn holes in the carpet and my mother's books were covered in sawdust, but nothing mattered anymore, so long as we stayed alive.

After Naomi and Eli had cut a tree into logs, I would take these out into the yard in an old laundry basket to split them length-wise into smaller bits for the stove. I chopped wood every day for an hour or so and quite liked the sense of accomplishment, relishing the way the hatchet would slice through a clear, knot-less log as a knife through butter. But at the same time I resented *having* to do it. After mother and Lena had left on their foraging trip, I felt a grave responsibility to keep the home-fires burning. With the authority of one left in command of a ship, I bullied Eli and Naomi, and Joe when he was strong enough, into cutting up all of the trees hauled with the help of the kerosene men. And I kept splitting the logs until they were gone, so that when the women came back, there was still enough wood for weeks.

## WOODS OPERATIONS II
(*Eli*)

Look
this woman
my small soft woman
hauling logs from a wheelbarrow
through French doors
into the backroom
each log crashing
to the floor just inside
as her arms give out
but never too soon.

Look
the sawhorse
wearing holes in the carpet
digging in its heels.

> Shapiro and I
> lift the logs
> onto the horse
> grunting and straining
> saw short chunks
> sweaty and panting.

Look
this thin child
my soft woman's tough snippet
takes the chunks outside
and splits them
all afternoon.

Our fire warms the holes
in the carpet
in my soft woman
in her tough child
in our hands
our nerves. And

look
these are facts.
No repair, no solution.

At night we reach out
and hold what we dream
in our aching arms.

## THE HUNGER TRIP

The day mother and Lena left we all got up before dawn to see them off. The two women each wore a pair of Wil's old hiking boots. That made them look like Mickey and Minnie Mouse, particularly Lena, who wore stockings and a skirt with one of my mother's warm woollen skipper's sweaters from her sailing days with my father. Lena was fashion-conscious and could still not ignore the pre-war Paris dictates: women do not wear trousers. Mother cared for no such directives and wore a pair of Eli's pants, gathered at the waist with Wil's cub belt – she was that thin – and tucked into the tops of the boots at the ankle. Both had big canvas saddlebags across their luggage carriers and in them they carried whatever there was in the house that might be of interest to the farmers. They had several sets of new underwear, left by Nurse Oppen, socks we had knitted, a few pieces of my mother's little cache of soap, and all the surrogate coffee we had been able to save up over the months. The surrogate coffee was made of roast acorns, ground with chicory, and tasted worse than hot water to us, but we had heard that with milk and sugar it was drinkable, and the farmers had milk as well as the sugar they made themselves from sugar beets. After kisses and embraces the women set off in the half-light and the rest of us went back to bed to keep warm a little longer.

My mother and Lena took the trip one day at a time. They knew someone near Putten, through friends, and were certain they could spend the first night there. Beyond that they had to take their chances. When at noon they saw smoke from a farmhouse chimney, they knew that dinner was being served, so they'd knock and would almost always get a bowl of porridge or pea soup. When instead they were given some slices of brown bread with bacon drippings they would stash them away to take home.

Beyond the river IJssel they began to have some success with their trading: they exchanged the clothing and the imitation coffee for wheat, rye, oats, dried peas and beans, a side of bacon, smoked pork, a chicken, a bottle of milk. Their bikes were groaning under the load when they started back. To avoid having to cross the bridge at Deventer, where the police sometimes made people give up what they had gathered, mother and Lena chose to cross the IJssel by ferry, a few miles to the south. They took the wrong turnoff once, and got stuck in the snow. Mother told us later that at that point she felt so tired and so despondent she would as soon have sat down in the snow and given up, and Lena had not felt much better.

However, the thought of us waiting at home made them struggle back up the dyke and finally they found the little ferry, barely more than a flat-bottomed boat. And on the ferry dock stood a guard of the *Grüne Polizei!*

My mother told Lena to sit down and wait while she chatted up the officer. She told him that she and her friend over there wanted to cross, that the friend was ill and was resting a bit. Then she asked the guard what part of Germany he came from and he told her, Rothenburg. She nodded and said she'd been there with her parents when she was a child. Did he have a wife there, and kids? Stuff like that. Finally she said, "Well, my friend must be rested by now, I'll go get her." But when the two women came down to the dock, ten minutes later, there had been a change of guards. With their hearts in their boots they wheeled their bicycles onto the ferry, but the new guard merely shook his head at the clumsy way they had tied up their bags, and patiently helped them to bind them up again more securely.

Once on the other side of the river, the trip back was along the open highway. RAF and RCAF Spitfires were strafing German trucks and other rolling stock frequently. When that happened, mother and Lena had to drop their bikes and jump into the manholes at the side of the road, along with dozens of other women with their children who were on hunger trips themselves. Cries of fear, the groaning of makeshift carts and wheelbarrows, the crying of the children and their own constant tense watchfulness made the journey a nightmare.

They slept in haystacks, or in barns, or sometimes in the attic of a farmhouse, but wherever they stayed, there never seemed an opportunity to wash. The pump was always in the yard where the hired hands were passing back and forth, and they dared not ask for a pail. But as they afterward reflected, the worst thing about the trip had been their need to be ruthless and single-minded about getting home with their loot without sharing with anyone else. That scared them, their complete lack of concern for anyone else, man, woman, or child. Nothing mattered but to get home, to survive and get home, in the shortest possible time.

No words can describe the reception at home. Joe could not stand up and had to sit on the lower stairs, holding hands with Lena, pulling her down on his lap, and she, torn between instinct and propriety, half bent over him, half knelt, with her cheek against his. And my mother, her back against the door, looking from Eli beside her to me at the top of the stairs, too tired to move in either direction, and only able to whisper, "I want a bath." Naomi and I sat there in silence, looking down at the women, and then at each other, thinking that we did not really see what we saw, and yet knowing exactly, storing all of it up in our hearts against future hunger.

## FIFTY-FIVE SOCKS

That last winter of war had its compensations.
We had no food except turnips and tulip bulbs.
But we did have a white knitted bedspread.

Barter was now the only thing, but who would want
a bridal bedspread when even the most essential clothing
could not be had for love nor money.
Who had love to spare anyway – survival was all.

The four of us, female, two Jewish, one gentile,
and one ignorant child, attacked the bedspread
early one morning in the room at the back.
In six days we knitted from its crinkled unravellings
fifty-five socks. That finished the cotton.

The socks folded neatly in pairs, the mateless one
in her pocket, my mother set out on a tireless bike
to trade with the farmers. None wanted socks
but finally at dusk one well-fed woman warmly dressed,
arms akimbo, was ready for business.

A side of bacon, two dozen eggs, five pounds of wheat
and a scruffy chicken bought her the socks.
Then my mother remembered the lonely extra
and would throw it in for a quart of milk
if the farmer's wife wanted.

Oh yes, she confessed, in a whispering voice, she wanted. She did not need socks, but she planned to unpick them, for she loved to knit and her heart was set on a lacy white bedspread.

## NO WATER

Spring came early that year but the weather remained cool and we still needed the heat of the stove, particularly at night, so the chopping still had to be done. Thanks to the food Lena and my mother had gathered together we had made it this far. Mother said she felt like a quartermaster, being so strict and doling out the food in very small portions.

With the coming of spring, Eli and I had begun to take cold showers in the morning and felt virtuous and superior about our cleanliness. The rest of the family felt that they did not need this sort of self-flagellation and used water heated on the back of the stove until even this last luxury fell away because the water supply itself was cut off. After that we had to get the water, one pail at a time, from a pump in the park and Eli's and my Spartan showers were a thing of the past.

The flowering crab and almond blossomed abundantly in the park as if nothing was wrong. Though the low iron rails and wrought-iron benches had long been converted into rifles and guns, and the work crews had long ago been sent to Germany to work, the old parks supervisor still came around to shoo away kids playing on the grass. But he came on foot now, and with less conviction, it seemed. The two ponds, emptied for winter as usual, remained empty all spring and only a clutch of last fall's beech leaves twirled around and around at the bottom.

## PUMP IN A DUTCH PARK

This is the fifth year of war
the last cold spring.
We are almost finished
doing without
heat   light   food

But water, not having it
no rush when you turn the faucet
not being able to wash
that is indignity.

Some municipal someone
has ordered a well to be sunk
in the nearby park. We can
fetch a pail of water
every morning, each night.

Sent with a bucket
half my size
I stand in line.
Later my mother will come
to carry it home between us.

The line snakes forward
splitting left, right
ahead, and back on itself
after the pump has delivered.
The faces are all the same –
papery, crumpled.

Four ahead of me, three ahead, two
then something snaps inside –
a washer gives out.
And I sit down hugging
the cold galvanised pail
and cry, telling myself
it is only water.

## STRAW
(*Mother*)

The last spring of war

I find my child in the park
disconsolate for failing
to get the morning's ration
of water from a broken pump.
She cries into her empty pail.

Through my tired mind shrugs
the parade of buckets
that mark this war for me:

Pails carrying furtive soup
from a central kitchen
to four illegal mouths
shut up in my backroom.

Pails in the corners
of cattle cars
on their way east.

Pails to swill sidewalks
after still another
public execution.

Impatiently I pull up the child
with one hand, with the other
lift the empty pail

and suddenly know
its dead weight
heavy as a last straw.

NO HOPE

Two hundred turns of the handle to grind and regrind the wheat and the rye in the coffee mill. Standing in line for water morning and night. The never-ending need for split firewood. The cutting of torches for our light at night with a blunt saw getting caught in the hardboard, and Eli giving edgy instructions behind me how you should pull, not push down on the saw. All of this accumulated into resentment and hopelessness. My anger should have been directed at Hitler of course, but he wasn't there in person, so instead it was turned more often onto the members of our cramped and churning little household.

All this must have been hard on my mother, too, but she never said anything. Before the war she had had an easy life, alone with Wil and me, and she could spend her days pretty much as she pleased – reading or sewing, writing letters or gardening. She had had help and could send out the laundry. But now that we were poor, there was no time for reading and the laundry had to be done by hand in lukewarm water with very little soap. And aside from that physical work there was the constant fear of being discovered, betrayed by a neighbour, arrested, deported – and what would happen to Wil and Maria if the Germans should find her out and put her up against the wall?

Whatever her fears, she kept them to herself. Even if she had wanted to stop, even if she had decided the stress was too great, at this point there was nothing she could do. She was a prisoner of the situation, as well as of her conscience and of her compassion and of her own pride too, I think.

## BARBERS

A Jew kept a store in a small Russian town, goes the story. His best friend was a Christian and they had been close friends for many years. One day the gentile came to call and found the Jew boarding up his windows.
— *What are you doing?* he asked.
— *I'm closing my business, I'm leaving,* his friend replied.
— *But why?*
— *I have heard there are going to be pogroms here against Jews and barbers.*
— *What?* cried the gentile, *Barbers?*

What, barbers? we all
fell into that trap

but not my mother, even then
wide awake, fiercely living
near losing her life
alone in her absolute knowing.

She was my centre
of blind gravitation.
I knew she was right
just by watching the tilt
of her chin.

Peace never offered such convictions.

## THE NEWS AS WE WANTED IT TO BE

One late afternoon in early May, Marion and I met once again on our island in the park. We hadn't been there for months. The empty ponds made it less of an island than it used to be and it was easy to stay out of the superintendent's sight, for the shrubs and bushes had not been pruned or trimmed and the new growth of leaves offered plenty of protection. Marion had good news: her father had heard from an acquaintance – who had heard it from a neighbour with an illegal radio receiver – that the allied forces were really on their way, had crossed the big rivers and could be here any day.

We must have looked a sight, two thin little girls in old, much-mended clothes, none too clean, squatting down between the white and red of flowering spirea and weigelia, discussing the likelihood of liberation. I earnestly told Marion that "we shouldn't believe everything we hear, you know, nor everything we read in *The Nutshell,* just because we want it to be so." But Marion's spirits were soaring too high to be pulled down by my borrowed wisdom, and in the end she convinced me that things were so bad now, they simply *had* to get better.

And in bed that night, listening to the faint sound of air raid sirens far away, I gave up thinking of Jesus. Instead I thought about vague but sturdy young soldiers who spoke the language of Virginia Woolf and D.H. Lawrence, and who let you stay out in the park after curfew.

In *The Nutshell* we had read that the provinces south of the big rivers had been liberated, and rumours like the one with which

Marion had cheered me on the island reached us repeatedly. The allied forces were advancing, but they weren't near enough yet for us to hear the battle and we didn't know what to believe. There was bombing and shooting in the city every day, and the air raid sirens sounded frequently, sometimes because "enemy" airplanes were overhead, and sometimes merely because the Germans wanted the civilians off the streets. Though all of that was scary, it meant something real was brewing at last.

One sunny morning, standing in line with my pail and waiting for water from the pump under the flowering almonds I heard the news: the Canadians were coming! The news travelled fast through the line-up. They were near – they would be there the next morning! Some people went home and came back again with orange or red-white-blue buttons in their lapels, to lend credence to the rumours. Just before curfew that evening our little courier with the Boy Scout scarf came with her friend who worked on *The Nutshell* and they confirmed it: there was going to be a chiefs-of-staff meeting the very next day, outside our town. Prince Bernhard would be there, and it was just a matter of negotiation. The streets were full of people. Nobody paid attention to the curfew, and mother decided that now it had been enough, now we could all go out. Lena and Joe did not dare go further than once around the park, for Joe still had trouble with his fainting spells. Naomi took off on her own, to meet a girlfriend who was also hiding in Amersfoort. And mother, Eli, and I walked up the hill to Eva's house to share the excitement.

Mother had given me permission to take Eva and her parents in my confidence, but this was the first chance my mother had to actually thank Eva's parents personally for their hospitality to me, and to explain her own apparent lack of hospitality. It was also the first time she introduced Eli to outsiders as her future husband and she was nervous about that, but nobody paid much attention as our minds were more on the public excitement of the impending liberation than on the private excitement of a wedding in the family.

Eva's father went to the cellar and brought out a bottle of wine, especially saved for the occasion. After that, the discussion of the news became less and less rational and analytic, until in the end we simply knew for sure that the news was finally what we wanted it to be. To settle the matter, Eva's brother Bob called from upstairs: "Hey! Come and watch this!" We ran up to the attic and from the window we saw the war end, not more than twenty kilometres away!

## STARS

From the attic window we could see the firing lines.
The Canadians were lighting flares / bright red
and green stars chased one another to the moon
slowed down / dipped in a gentle arc to explode
one by one into smaller stars / then still smaller ones
in our eyes. Why did we cry?
"Do they care so much for us then, that they're
letting us know it's all over?" I asked my mother.
She might have laughed / might have pointed out
that those boys were also tired / also happy
to stop doing without. But she nodded,
squeezed my arm and did not touch
my starry eyes.

THE FIRST DAY OF PEACE

Joe and Lena had already left. Naomi was nowhere to be found.
Eli, mother, and I walked downtown slowly, tasting the unusual.
It was a crazy thing for Eli, unreal in the sun.
But I couldn't look at Eli and my mother, holding hands
   in bright daylight.

We lined up along the main street for the parade. It was
a broad street. (Not true, I went back there – two cars
can barely pass.) We waited with upturned faces.

    German officers kept back the crowd –
    a last nod at discipline.

An elderly man jumped up high to flick a swinging shingle.
Two girls waltzed on the sidewalk to inward music. Friends
hugged old winter-lost friends. Mother held onto Eli. Eli
   searched
the crowd apprehensively for survivors. All around was laughter
and the excited murmur of expectancy.

    *Sie lachen noch wenn die Russen kommen!*
    snarled a white-faced officer.
    *Ja!* roared the crowd.

Hours passed. Then two Canadian couriers rumbled down
   the road
tanned and sunbleached, straddling the tanks of their motor
   bikes, way up front.

Very special we thought. Very Canadian we thought
though no one had ever seen a Canadian before.

The riders stopped in the marketplace and squinted over their
shoulders at the troops they expected, but nothing followed.
Shrugging, they grinned at each other and at that sign of
humanity the crowd pushed the shrivelled Germans out of the
way and mobbed the two Canadians, lifting them high on their
shoulders, and carried them off God knows where.

> Two German soldiers rescued the bikes, placing
> them neatly side by side in the courtyard of
> the police bureau.

We walked home. In a sleepy street an old man
came slowly out of his house and asked,
"Could you tell me please what is going on?"
"The war is over!!"
"Oh, thank you," he muttered vaguely,
and shuffled back inside.

## BREAD AND MARGARINE

The days that followed were incredible. Suddenly all prohibitions were gone: no curfew, no secrets to keep, warm weather and no wood to chop, the windows and doors wide open from morning till night. We could say what we wanted, read what we wanted, speak to anyone, make noise, let on the house was full of people. And above all, the cold no longer forced us to stay in the one room.

Our first hunger was alleviated by the bread and margarine sent by the Swedish Red Cross. Just before the end, in early May when the Germans secretly knew the game was up, they had allowed the Red Cross to drop off food for the starving population from low-flying planes. Eva and I went to see how it was done. There was a municipal sports park west of town – a huge complex of dozens of soccer and field hockey grounds. The fences separating the fields, and the wooden goal posts, had long since been translated into fuel for people's stoves and the planes could easily fly low over the ground and drop the large grey parcels of food, then ascend again. There were two planes, each taking its turn dropping a dozen or so parcels, then regaining altitude, circling, and coming down again to drop more parcels, exactly as we had seen the bombers swoop down on the shunting yards north of the city.

The parcels were taken to the central distribution office where the ration coupons had been handed out all through the war, and from there they were distributed to the stores. Instead of oil and sour potato-bread we could now get Swedish white bread and margarine, free of charge, in exchange for our coupons. The bread was whiter than pre-war bread could ever have been, and the margarine tasted better than the best quality butter. The Red Cross aid came through just about the day the war ended. Slowly the stores began to fill up again, first with fresh fruit and vegetables that were no longer whisked off to Germany, then with dairy products, and later still with baked and processed food. Even so, everything was still in short supply and remained rationed for quite some time after the war was over.

SONGS AND TOMATOES

The summer of 1945 was glorious. The sun seemed to shine every day, and everything that happened, in the streets, in the park, in the house and later, back in school, was exciting. The full richness of life came crashing home to all of us, so eager were we to put the war behind us.

That we had been starved for more than food was never so clear as in the first person-to-person encounters with our liberators. Canadian soldiers were billeted in schools and in empty houses, as well as in the homes of some lucky citizens who had room to spare. The Hansens had been ousted from their home by the new Dutch authorities and put in a detention camp before being repatriated to Germany, their country, where they had not lived for forty years and where they would not be welcome. But we felt no sympathy for them. In their house now lived half a dozen Canadian officers and they were wonderful.

*All* Canadians were wonderful, by definition. They were witty, clever, they spoke a fascinating language, wore impressive uniforms, smiled radiant smiles, left trails of cigarettes and Lifesavers. They were creatures from another world, bringing plenty and good cheer. Even the songs they sang belonged to another world. Three of the men in the Hansens' house loved singing and came out on the sidewalk every evening, one with a ukulele. The first evening Marion, Eli, and I sat on the fence, just watching and listening. Other neighbours and passers-by stopped and in no time the singers had an audience. The first song they sang was "Swinging on a Star." Its sheer silliness was a breath of fresh air and, more than willing to be entertained, we were delighted out of all proportion to the merits of the song. After that they sang songs like "Home on the Range" and "Don't Fence Me In" and "Sentimental Journey" but it was the "animal with long funny ears" we carried home – moonbeams in a jar.

Of course we came down from that star, settled down to plain living, but never merely *went back* to it. For a long time we took nothing for granted. The first fresh tomato seemed a miracle. Years later I read a book of prose-poems, written by a prisoner in the camp on 1914 Avenue, who had used his imagination as a defence against the spirit-breaking prison life, and the way he *remembered* a tomato was not far from the way we *re-experienced* it:

## TOMATO[2]

Tomato: tomato-red and yellow; no, not orange, not red, but tomato-red, tomato-red-orange with yellow, yellowish specks invisibly small in that red, no, that tomato-red.
Nip the skin with your teeth, catch it, it peels, it curls off, becomes tissue-thin peel.
Underneath: the tomato, the soft berry-red tomato flesh, clashing with the hue of the peel, already withered. Tomato meat, naked, hurts the eye, tender as a wound.
Dare to bite in. Here are the compartments, pinkish and yellowish, fresh and firm, tartly dividing the soft flesh.
    Feels like the roof of your mouth.
Between the partitions the liquid, the softest tomato-jelly, the slippery bed where the yellow pips, the seeds, swim in rows, lie bathed, bedded-down – an intimate secret.
At the top of the tomato, a shrivelled bouquet, shielding the yellowish scar: spiky olive-green leaves.
Tomato.
Sunjuicefruit.
Sunjuice.
Sun.

MY MOTHER AND I ESCAPE AGAIN

The surprised eye that we now brought to everyday things made that first post-war summer one grand celebration. Sometimes the fullness of every day was almost too much to bear and we could not cope with anything that came on top of it, as when there was going to be a big parade of troops and war equipment on the moors south of town. But mother and I had ways to deal with that: I stayed home and closed all the doors and windows. And my mother escaped in her own way.

## CELEBRATION
(*Eli*)

A few weeks after the end of the war
there was to be a parade, a demonstration
of war machines in action. We adults
went to see what had won the war.

And this is what happened
A child played with her doll's house
alone at home where the sound and colour
of her own thoughts made her blind and deaf.

This is what happened
Martial music was drowned by tanks
tearing up tarmac. The horrible heart-thump
of bazookas was shouted down by the shrieking
blaze from flame throwers. Noise and heat
and ghastly iron masqueraded as festive.

And this is what happened
this is what happened
My small gentle woman
asleep by the roadside
throughout
the entire celebration.

We had to shake her
to make her believe
it was over.

## WHAT HAPPENED NEXT

Wil came home and brought his girl Christien. We loved her straightaway, and though perhaps she felt a little overwhelmed by her boyfriend's unusual family, she became part of it easily enough. My uncle Jan and his family and *their* two hidden friends made it through the war safely but he went into a tailspin of exhaustion and depression, and it was months before he recovered and the connection was re-established. Lena and Joe moved into the Hansens' house after the Canadians left. Their little girl Lisa, for whom Lena had knitted the dresses and bloomers, came back to live with her unfamiliar parents again, God knows at what cost to the child and to her foster mother of three years. The next spring Lena had a new baby, but not long after that Joe died of diabetes and Lena and her children moved back to Amsterdam where she had grown up, and we never heard from her again.

Of Naomi's relatives, only one of her brothers returned from the camps, and Naomi herself emigrated to Israel as soon as she saw her way clear. Many years later she visited Holland with her husband and came to see my mother in her "elastic" house as she used to call it. She still lives in Israel and we have kept in touch.

It is strange that I remember nothing whatever of our friends' receiving confirmation of their relatives' deaths, though they must have received it around this time. When did the suspicion of what happened in Bergen-Belsen and Dachau, Buchenwald and Treblinka, become public knowledge? How did Eli and Naomi, Joe and Lena take it? I don't remember. Either I have pushed away the memory or they kept their grief from our incomprehension and mourned their dead in solitude.

In time a letter came from my father to say he was coming back to Holland and would visit us as soon as he could. Once I knew what hour his train would arrive, I prepared for his coming by trying on new outfits from a box of hand-me-downs a friend of my mother's had sent us. The clothes were of very good quality but unlike any I had ever owned. My choice fell on a white organza dress that I thought would be smashing. Unused to the sheer fabric of such a party dress, I was unaware that it required a white slip to go underneath. When the doorbell rang I rushed down the stairs in my gossamer attire, and flung myself into my father's arms, my sturdy knitted underwear providing a lovely distraction and a source of laughter for all the family, easing what might have been a tense reunion.

My father brought us a huge tin of preserved peaches – the kind they use on board ship to feed the entire crew – and we ate peaches every day for a week. He was in his early fifties then, but the war had aged him and I couldn't believe that he had been my mother's husband. I instantly loved him again, and precisely because of that I felt extra guilt that I secretly thought Eli more suitable to be married to my pretty young-looking mother.

Eli and mother got married that summer and were very happy until well after I left home, seven years later. I would not say that Eli and I always hit it off very well together. We vied fiercely with one another for my mother's attention, and as I entered a late adolescence it seemed less and less obvious to me why Eli should exercise the authority that I had easily accepted when I was a child. But underneath these tensions we retained good feelings, and I guess none of us ever forgot the real source of strength we had been to each other in the years of oppression we left further and further behind us. Writing from Israel where he lived for a time, Eli said as much. Though his letter was addressed to me, it was intended for all, and I include it here in translation.

## OPEN LETTER TO MARIA, JERUSALEM, 1978[3]
*(Eli)*

Maria
Jacob slept at Peniel.
He woke up with an old grey guilt.

Your mother
the small woman in the narrow house
went her own unnoticed way.
She saved a handful of lives
a dozen or so
in passing.
Her name is recorded nowhere.

You
the little snippet
easily carried a weighty secret
and firewood so heavy
I could not lift it.
Your thin arms
strong as your will
fetched the daily pailful of food
for the boarders
who held no title to their lives.

But I
the grown man
did not remain idle.
I made you a doll's house

while my sisters just died
in the shower rooms.

There are oceans between us
between then and now.
Sometimes we meet for an hour
in the narrow house.
We see the roof
untouched.

Maria, that Jacob – remember? –
fought with the angel
a lifelong night
and injured his hip.
For years now
his name has been Israel.

We are scattered in all directions now, but the roof of the house we made for each other is still intact. My mother is old and frail, Eli's hair is grey, and geographically they live far apart, but in the spirit they are still close and the warmth and solidarity between them will not be destroyed.

I have a life and a family of my own now that have little connection with the life we lived then. I live in the country that shone for us like a bright star. I speak the language that fascinated us so much and that has since become more my own in many respects than the one we spoke when we lived our war and took our precautions. But the language my mother speaks to Eli and me is the same one Eli speaks to us, and it is the same I speak to them: it has no sound.

# CODA

TWENTY YEARS LATER

Twenty years ago, when this book was first published, the events that inspired it had themselves occurred forty years earlier. I was barely more than a child then, twelve, thirteen years old, and though very much alive to the facts of those turbulent years, it would not be until much later that I had the perspective to make sense of their ramifications.

Now I have gained even further insight into those times, and have seen more human beings destroying their fellow human beings. I know that no one lives long enough to get the full picture of Hitler's legacy, if only because the horrors of fascism continue – perhaps under different banners, to different groups, perpetrated by different people – but they continue. Even so, I want to complete the story of my own family as far as I can, because for all that was lost to my mother, Eli, Naomi, Lena and Joe, my brother, myself, more was gained – a certain knowledge that the forces of good sometimes win out over the forces of evil, however narrowly, however randomly, however infrequently.

After the liberation of The Netherlands by the Canadians, food became available again. We regained our strength and resilience, and I quickly grew up. I began to blossom, as my grandmother put it when she studied my contours in a too-tight outgrown sweater. By the time I turned fifteen in the fall of 1945, I had, at least on the surface, become a young woman, though it would take awhile for my soul to catch up with my body.

When my mother and Eli decided to get married that very year, their plan met with some raised eyebrows, as he was 17 years younger than she, and even her brother Jan, who understood her well and was not narrow-minded, felt he had to warn her. She must realise, he said, that in another fifteen years she would be an old woman while Eli would still be in the prime of life. She thought about that carefully, but her longing for an end to care and suffering and a start to new happiness made her reply that "Yes, I know it may not last, but I will have this now, and I'm going to risk it." This was completely in tune with her earlier reckless decision to enter the fray against fascism. The marriage lasted ten happy, then turbulent and ultimately difficult years, before she lost her restless, nervous husband to a younger woman. By that time I had married, and left the country with my new husband, so I only heard intermittently, through letters and when visiting my mother, what had happened and how it had affected her. At first it had been sheer hell, she said, but with time she became reconciled to her single status and she never regretted her years with Eli. And though later she had several offers, she never married again.

※

With puberty, "men" became an issue for me. Of course I already had my brother Wil, and Eli, and my uncle Jan, and my dad, but now my eye began to be drawn to outsiders. First of all the handsome, well-fed, sunburnt young Canadians who had liberated us from the dark cold winter caught my fancy, and I made up my mind to marry one of them and emigrate to Canada. But that was a passing ambition. I had some more growing up to do, and in time high school and skating, field hockey and sailing offered plenty of exposure to a series of more suitable boys.

One of these pressed his advantage to great effect. Peter and I were married in 1953 and emigrated to the U.S. A couple of years later, we moved to Canada, the country that had cast such an irresistible spell over so many of us after the war. It turned out to be a good decision, as we felt at home and did well in our adopted country. We both acquired a university education and in the interstices had five healthy children. I could write several books about that giddy and exciting time of discovery and adjustment, but in this book let me stay a little closer to the aftermath of the German occupation of my home country and how it affected my offspring.

※

Our five children were a delight to us, and to each other most of the time, and they still are. As they grew up they did not know much about the Second World War, although there was much to know. My husband had not been in Europe during that time but lived with his family in Indonesia, where for three years he languished in a Japanese prisoner-of-war camp on Java. Peter would never speak of that experience, and even today is not forthcoming about it.

It seemed to take time to get round to examining our early life, particularly since it had been such a troubled time for both of us. My own decision to break the silence was fortuitous. I had begun to write poetry and, as writers do, I cast about for subject matter. One spring day in the seventies, the warm air suddenly reminded me of an incident in another spring, more than 30 years before, just before the liberation. It inspired "Burnt buttercups," the poem on page 43 above. After that, another poem sprang up, and another, and when I had written a dozen or so, I thought I had said everything I had to say about that time. The poems were published in *CV II*[4] and glowingly commented upon by Dorothy Livesay.[5] This gave me tremendous courage, enough to send them off to a publisher, who in fact decided to publish the book that became *Precautions Against Death*.

When the page proofs of my book arrived, I engaged my two young daughters (18 and 21 years old at that time) as proofreaders, because there were time constraints as the proofs had to be returned within 4 days. It woke the girls up with a jolt. Suddenly *The Diary of Anne Frank,* which they had read and discussed in junior high school, was no longer just a dark story, but a real-life horror, to which my book became a kind of counterpoint.

From a production point of view, our communal proofreading turned out to be futile, as our corrections somehow did not make it to the typesetter and the book appeared with a shocking number of errors and typos. But from a personal point of view it was a great success. My daughters made their brothers all read the book, and once they had read it, all began to ask questions and received answers. In time my children-in-law and later still my grandchildren also read the book, asked more questions, and received more answers. Not ultimate answers, just the piecemeal answers I felt qualified to give. I hope, or rather know, that every one of my offspring and grand-offspring has taken away something of my mother's courage.

⁂

But I am getting ahead of myself. Even though my husband and I did not speak much about our disparate wartime experiences, this did not mean that the children were not aware of the dangers of racism, or any kind of "ism." Their father and I would not tolerate any kind of racist joke or expression the children brought home from school, and we made it clear why not. We did not sit them down and lecture to them, but dealt with racist expressions as they cropped up.

One day in early winter, when the girls were 10 and 13, we were beginning to prepare for Christmas. We had just finished decorating an oddly shaped branch of a tree, hung with stars and three small gold crowns. We were not religious – the crowns merely represented the three legendary kings who "from Orient are." Anne saw them clearly as symbols, and recognised their dark aspects. Her younger sister saw beyond the Christian tradition and realised their legitimacy as well. Then the phone rang, and here's what ensued:

## A KOSHER LUNCH[6]

Almost Christmas and my girls
dress a weird twisted branch
cut from a lovely old tree
with bells, bright stars
and three gilt crowns.

Then the phone surprises
with friends from New York
tomorrow for lunch. They are
orthodox Jews and the girls and I
sit down to plan the meal.

Lox and bagels, kosher cream cheese
and dills, home-made butter cake
tea in glasses
paper napkins and plates: ah –
our finesse will make them smile
the way the Dutch roll their eyes
at the mention of windmills
and wooden shoes.

Next day, the table set,
Anne, thirteen, surveys
the welcoming room
with her warm brown eyes
and supposes *it's best
to remove those crowns
from that branch.*

But the golden one, ten,
lifts up her clear head
grey gaze on her sister
and asks, pensively,
*but do they take off
their yarmulkes
when we come to visit?*

Textbook examples
my two fair daughters
empathy and reason
and I need not take sides.

I'll never forget how this small exchange of opinions thrilled me. Had my mother's legacy passed through me to them? I can't remember discussing anti-Semitism as such with them beyond the standing rule that racist jokes were out. And perhaps Dr. Seuss's Star-bellied Sneetches had left their imprint? Whatever prompted their reaction, it gave me confidence that if they are ever faced with a situation like the one that faced my mother, their choices will be informed.

◈

After *Precautions Against Death* came out, I was frequently asked to give talks about our wartime experiences at high schools and to groups studying the Holocaust. Once when I talked to a group of junior high school students, one little girl asked if, when I was in high school, we had had designer clothes! This caused some tittering, and after I replied that we counted ourselves lucky to have clothes of any kind, the teacher decided to end the discussion with a weightier question. She asked me if I had not loathed the Nazis, and also if I had not resented my mother's decision to do this work, as it basically must have robbed me of my childhood. Her words stunned me, much more than the last student's question. *That* question, after all, had come straight from her identification with the girl I must once have been, and reflected her own present preoccupation. But the teacher's question amazed me. Had I somehow failed to convey the enormous emotional strength of the friendship that grew in our incongruous "family" during those days and months of enforced proximity and shared fears? Or was she, also, speaking from some private preoccupation?

The entire enterprise during the war had made me realise that I had a mother out of a million, one with enough courage to take on fascism single-handed. I had discovered the spunk my young brother Wil had brought to the enterprise. I found close and trusted friends in Naomi and Eli, and, personalities to one side, even Lena and Joe became intimately connected. These were people we would not have met and loved under normal circumstances and who went on to play major roles in our lives. Rather than resenting and hating our circumstances, I grew up to value this period in my life for all that it brought and taught.

As far as loathing the Nazis went, that question required no affirmation. In this respect we had plenty of company, after five years under their boot and experiencing their ruthlessness. Yet even this aspect of the war had had its positive effect. After witnessing anti-Semitism-in-action, racism would be unlikely to gain a foothold in my mind, although my mother's free and spirited views on the matter would have made that unlikely in any case.

OUR TRIP TO JERUSALEM

For a number of years my own life and family was taking all my attention and energy away from my parental family, and my contact with Eli and Naomi had become tenuous. But as the children grew up and I could take time to visit my mother more frequently, we got in touch again. In 1983 Eli and Naomi began to hatch a plot and they asked us if we would come to Jerusalem to be honoured by Yad Vashem, and to plant a tree on the "Avenue of the Righteous Gentiles," because they wanted to make sure that our names would be recorded.

The ceremony would take place at Yad Vashem, the organisation charged with honouring both the victims and those who were instrumental in saving the lives of Jews persecuted under the Nazi regime in Europe. Though seeing Jerusalem had been a long-cherished wish, my mother initially declined, saying, "Oh nonsense, so many of us did that during the war – it had to be done, it was nothing special." But of course it *had* been special, and Wil and I encouraged her to accept the invitation, if not for herself, then for her grandchildren and great-grandchildren, and also to respect Naomi's and Eli's desire to honour her. We convinced her, and our travel plans got underway. Eli and Naomi would put us up and look after us once we got to Israel, and they paid my mother's fare. Wil wanted to bring his wife Christien, and they would pay their own way, but the return fare from Canada was expensive, and beyond our means, so initially it looked like I would not be able to go. But through a good friend with business connections, word was sent out among the Jewish business community in Toronto, and its members generously paid for my return fare to Israel.

So we did go. Eli put up my mother and me in his small apartment in Gilo, then a peaceful, now a turbulent suburb of Jerusalem. Naomi's sister, Lottie, who had immigrated to Palestine before the war, lived in Jerusalem and was glad to put up Wil and Christien. Naomi and her husband Niso lived in

Ramle, between Tel Aviv and Jerusalem, and it was there that our little convoy and our hosts first met again after all these years. What a reunion that was! I can't imagine a more cordial and happy reception than the one we received.

The communal meal we enjoyed that night was only the beginning. Everything had been planned with the utmost care, trips had been scheduled, sight-seeing tours had been booked, Eli had even arranged for a wheelchair so that my elderly mother need not walk through hilly Jerusalem but could take everything in from the chair. Though he was now in his mid-sixties, Eli insisted on pushing and pulling her everywhere single-handed. He only allowed Wil to help him when the chair had to be lifted up or down flights of stairs, of which there were many, and in this way she saw every nook and cranny of that fascinating city.

The ceremony in the memorial hall at Yad Vashem was most impressive. The floor of the hall was paved with large flagstones, interspersed with metal plaques, each one carrying the name of one of the death camps. An eternal flame commemorating the dead was burning on the floor, like an open fire in the desert. The pitched wooden ceiling of the hall made us feel as if we were gathered in a large tent. The atmosphere seemed to be both one of sad serenity and quiet gratitude in looking back to the upheaval in Europe, many years ago, that was the reason for Yad Vashem's existence. We all felt it, and Mother, Wil and I were glad we had come and were deeply grateful to Eli and Naomi for bringing our shared history come full-circle. As we stood there quietly together for a time, I recalled Eli's open letter again,

"Your mother ... saved a handful of lives
a dozen or so
in passing.
her name is recorded nowhere."

It now is well and truly recorded.

From the memorial building we then proceeded to the Avenue of the Righteous. This was a sandy road lined with trees and trees "under construction," small saplings struggling to root. Each of these had been planted by or for a "righteous gentile" – one who had helped prevent the death of a Jew at the hand of Nazis. The group halted at a spot where a hole had been dug, and a tiny tree, its roots held in burlap, was waiting to be planted. Because of my mother's advanced age, Wil and I did the honours, and so our little tree became the newest addition to a long row.

After the ceremony, family and friends gathered at Lottie's home where she had prepared a lavish luncheon. Most of the people there were unknown to us, except by reputation, but they seemed like old friends, and my mother looked so happy and thoroughly fêted, it was a pleasure and honour to be there that day. Eli, who at that time had been in Israel for four years, was newly separated from his wife of several decades, but they remained friends, and she, too, was part of the party and got on very well with my mother. Eli was incapable of carrying grudges and did not bring them out in his wives.

The excursions that had been laid on for us took us to the Dead Sea, where we coasted on top of the water and took the requisite mud bath. From there we went to nearby Ein Gedi, an oasis in the desert, where one of the rare fresh water creeks comes down from the mountains to the sea. Another day we went to Nazareth in Galilee, and to the river Jordan. We saw the Mount of Olives, and Mary's tomb and the place where Christ was said to have been crucified, as well as his putative birthplace in Bethlehem. And we went to Caesarea, and to Akra, the fortification where the Crusaders wreaked havoc centuries ago. We climbed Masada, and we saw the remnants of the synagogue at Caphernaum, which we reached by boat across the Sea of Galilee. All these things were enormously meaningful and surprisingly moving. We were not religious, and had not expected to be excited by the Biblical significance of the country, but this was, after all, where our history began, for our hosts as well as for ourselves.

One day, on our way to Bethlehem, a hilarious incident occurred. We had stopped at the tomb of Rachel, housed in a small stone building, where a group of men were gathering to say prayers. There were eight men, and they frantically beckoned Eli and Wil to join them to make *minyan* (the requisite number of Jewish men for prayer). Eli went over, and tried to explain that my brother was not a Jew and did not qualify, but the men were unimpressed, one of them pulled a yarmulke out of his pocket, and planted it on Wil's head, and hey presto, he was drafted! He looked quite appropriate in his neat grey suit, and God surely must have accepted what was offered there in the way of prayer!

The year following our trip to Jerusalem that had been such a highpoint for all of us, Eli returned to Amsterdam. The transplantation to Israel had not "taken" – he felt too old to adapt to a new language, new customs, and new neighbours. It was almost as if welcoming us to Israel and the ceremony at Yad Vashem had been a sacred task for him, and he had stayed just long enough to bring it about.

For my mother, too, the visit had been a blessing. It made up for the many difficult episodes in her life, and in fact it was also the beginning of a renewed understanding between her and Eli. They had kept in touch over the years, but had not seen much of one another because he was resolved to make a good job of his new marriage and fatherhood. But after Jerusalem, after he returned to Holland, he began to see my mother again, not frequently but regularly, until her death.

During one of my stays to the Netherlands, two things happened that left an indelible impression, or perhaps depression is a better word. Eli came to visit us in my mother's apartment, and brought an Israeli friend, who talked about some of the things she remembered from her own time under the Nazis. She had been born in France and lived in Paris when the war broke out. She had been deported, and though she survived her internment, she was understandably still full of bitter anger. One of the things she had particularly resented was the fact that as a child she had not known the meaning of the word Jew. All she ever heard was "salejew" (dirtyjew), an appellation so common, she had thought it was one word, the only word pertaining to her people.

The other depressing thing I experienced on that visit was the television reportage of the trials of Majdanek, at which statements were taken from the guards and manager of that concentration camp. The television program took three days, and my mother, uncle Jan and I were totally mesmerised by the questioning of these people, and especially by their responses. One after another they were asked the same questions, and all made more or less the same replies: *We were instructed to do such and such, so we did it.* Their faces were expressionless, none showed sadness or remorse, or any feelings at all, nor did any of them show that they were proud of their acts or justified in what they had done. These were facts and they did not deny them, but feelings did not enter into the matter.

Although I had "known" what had happened in those camps, had read numerous books about it, and had heard many eyewitness accounts, hearing and seeing these dispassionate admissions over and over again was devastating. These people had lived with the knowledge of the suffering they had caused for over thirty years, and had inexplicably reconciled themselves to the role they had played in the deaths of thousands. I have often asked myself why we were so riveted to the television for three days. Perhaps we were hoping that we would glimpse some sign of regret, some recognition of guilt, just once in a while, but we were disappointed.

## EUROPE REVISITED[7]

Every time I go back the war catches me
from behind. A friend's new lover tells
how she grew up in France, ignorant
of the word *juif* – *salejuif* being familiar.
She was ten when the Nazis came
and her proud new period stopped.

We talked of nightmares, how they wake you
with a hammer, though science says the pounding
comes first, the dream follows in seconds
to fit the turbulence.

> In this dream they come back to the camp from the tavern
> eight guards – three women, five men. The women
> staggering under armfuls of flowers, the men merely
> staggering.
>
> Between the barracks a small girl nurses
> a doll, a white paper napkin folded for a cap, another
> tucked in her waistband for an apron.
>                          The women
> kneel and, cooing, place their flowers all round
> the little *salejuif,* like a halo, then
> step back to admire the effect.
>                          The men aim
> and empty their guns into nurse, doll and flowers.
> *Red periods stain the white apron.*

Science is right.
I made it up.
I was never there.
They didn't have white paper napkins then.
I am not writing this.

Sometime in the mid-eighties, I was asked to represent my mother – who by this time was too frail to travel – at a conference organised by the U.S. State Department in Washington. This conference was organised in honour of gentiles who had helped save the lives of Jews during the Nazi regime in Europe. It left a great impression on me, to be in the company of people from all over Europe who had been unanimous in their decision to resist Hitler's satanic plans.

At this conference, a sociologist from California, Sam Oliner, interviewed a large number of the guests to find out why they had risked their lives to save those of others. I had been asked that question many times, but to answer it on behalf of my mother was not possible. I could guess at it, but that was all. The interviewer asked the standard questions: *Had my mother had a strong faith that prompted her?* No, my mother was not religious, but yes, she was brought up in the Protestant faith and certainly knew right from wrong. *Did her decision injure me?* As it happened, we all made it through the occupation, and I felt in no way psychologically injured by our experience. *Did the experience affect my attitude vis-à-vis the Jews?* Yes, it did. Before the war I had not had any attitude – Jews were no different from any other people. Now that I was aware of them, and had come to know and love a number of them, I was more likely than not to be predisposed to like them. The irony here is, of course, that this, too, is a form of discrimination, albeit positive, so yes, the Nazi regime may be said to have brought that about in me, in reaction to their doctrines.

Another question that was frequently asked and which also occurred in Sam Oliner's interviews was, *If the situation came up again, would I conduct myself as she had done?* I honestly don't know. I hope so, but the situation would have to present itself before I could answer in the affirmative.

## WHEN THE SNOW LAY ROUND ABOUT[8]

in Washington
I am to talk about the holocaust
as though I knew.

        I am alive
and so are our survivors
the Jews my mother saved.
Sheer windfalls, folks we found
to love along the road.

        There's no
explaining fortune.

        What I want
explained to me is this,
my mother, why she did
all that I want reluctantly
to follow
        footsteps
                Wenceslas
in fear of death
        her page.

Much later, when the Persian Gulf War got underway in 1991, and missiles were fired at Israel from Iraq, it seemed for a while that an even more complex question had to be answered, which kept me awake many nights.

## THE PERSIAN GULF WAR[9]
(*For Naomi and Eli – 17 January 1991*)

If we were merely defending the right to take
hot showers twice a day or drive a car
I'd be marching along with the rest.

But two days into this war, and how can I not
defend your safety, the right to your country
and title to the lives you nearly lost?

The issue *then* was simple: Hitler sought
to take that title from you, and my mother
would not let him, acted secretly, not taking lives,
but shielding yours, hiding your very presence
in her small Dutch house.

I was so sure I could be strong as she
if called upon, but *now* it means
I'd have to vote for carpet-bombing
boys who did not vote their leader in
and have no choice but go in Allah's name
to the pain of their death.

I want to shield your lives as she once did
or else it will have been in vain, but *now*
it means I have to send the gentlest of my sons
whom I have taught the best peace that I know.

If this is courage, I'm afraid.

After returning to Canada from Israel, Holland, Washington, I began to realise how seemingly insignificant, small, everyday occurrences were coloured by my awareness of anti-Semitism, and by my suspicion that it was lurking everywhere, even in the vegetable section of the local supermarket:

## WHEN YOU'RE MAKING LATKES[10]

a potato with runes is unbelievable.
From a paper bag you pull a potato
showing a thumbnail sketch of a number sign
a plan for noughts and crosses
and on the other side a swastika

slaps you. You peel quickly, thickly
but it's still rotten to the core
pitch it
it was never there

a bored farmhand
someone using a nail on his lunch break
like spray paint stolen in New York
to decorate subways:
boredom.

whatever comes naturally:
I love P.E.I.
tic tac toe
*wolfsangel, hakenkreutz*
whatever focuses guts
in the break

thank God it was me who found
this crucified spud.

After I examined first my hot angry reaction and then the potato bag more closely, I realised that none of my suspicions was justified, that nobody had done racist graffiti on the potatoes. The ominous patterns were merely caused by the imprint of the small, net-covered peephole in the paper bag. I was relieved but also disturbed that my fury had only been one more little legacy of war.

After my mother came home from Israel, it seemed as though there was nothing more for her to wish for. She had done what she had to do, and had been recognised. Although she had not wanted "the hoopla," as she called it, it was very good that it had happened, for her, for Eli, for Naomi, and for us, her children.

At this time I decided to increase my visits to two a year. My favourite uncle Jan had lost his wife some years before, and lived very near, so my mother and he spent most evenings together, reading and talking, or watching television, while enjoying their habitual Scotch. They had been life-long friends, but their lives were coming to an end and there wasn't a lot left to say. When I visited, their evenings became a little more animated, because I brought new ideas, had read different books, was used to a different political climate, and in general provided a distraction.

It was at the end of one evening during a spring visit, that my mother tripped and fell while preparing for bed. She was in great pain, and judging from the angle of her leg, I feared the worst. The doctor came immediately and indeed confirmed a broken thighbone. Twenty minutes later she was in hospital, where the hip was operated upon the next day, but though the bone graft mended well, she never regained the full use of her leg, in spite of extensive physiotherapy. And we noticed that her mind began to wander. This was the beginning of the end.

Late April I left to go back to my family in Canada. Wil and Christien were towers of strength. They brought our mother to a nursing home in the town where they lived, north of Amsterdam, so that they could visit her daily. They did their utmost to arrange her new room exactly the way her old room had been in the smallest details, but she never really recognised the place as her own. At that time, Eli was living in Amsterdam and he took the train every week to bring her fruit, or a cold bottle of juice, or just to sit with her and read to her for a few hours. When I saw her again in August of that year, I found a confused and sad little bird, a mere shade of the strong woman she had been.

Saying goodbye at the end of that visit was one of the hardest things I have ever had to do, because I knew I would not see her alive and conscious again. Even now she was almost always sleeping or at least dozing, and barely reacted any longer when we spoke to her. The night before I was to return to Canada, I was alone with her, holding her hand for a long time, and though I tried to talk to her, the words had no sound.

When at last I put my arms around her and asked her to give me a hug, she turned her face toward me and said softly, *Oh – you poor girl*. I hoped she did not know how poor. But I think she knew how rich.

NOTES

1) p. 33

Shaddai, a name of the Almighty. The mezuzah, a small scrap of parchment on which the biblical texts Deuteronomy 6: 4–9 and 11: 13–31 are written, has the word Shaddai. The parchment is rolled in a cylindrical container, fastened to the doorframe as a sign that a Jewish family lives within. In *The Magician of Lublin,* I.B. Singer offers a loose translation of the name Shaddai: "The One Who said Enough" (*Dai* means enough in Hebrew).

2) p. 106

"Tomato" from *Verbeelding als wapen* (Imagination as weapon) by Floris B. Bakels, Elsevier, Amsterdam/Brussels, 1979, translated by Maria Jacobs.

3) p. 112

Although most of the poems gave voice to the *dramatis personae,* this is a literary device. "Open letter to Maria" is an exception. It was written by Eli under the pseudonym Menachem Mendel, and was reprinted by permission of the author.

4) p. 120

*CV II* Vol. 4 No. 2, Spring 1979

5) p. 120

*CV II* Vol. 4 No. 3, Fall 1979

6) p. 122
"A kosher lunch" from *What Feathers Are For* by Maria Jacobs, Mosaic Press, Oakville, ON, 1983.

7) p. 132
"Europe revisited" from *Iseult, We Are Barren* by Maria Jacobs, Netherlandic Press, Windsor, ON, 1987.

8) p. 136
"When the snow lay round about," from *Iseult, We Are Barren*.

9) p. 138
"The Persian Gulf War," from *A Discord of Flags*, a privately printed anthology of poems protesting the Gulf War in 1991, Steven Heighton, Peter Ormshaw, and Michael Redhill, eds. Toronto, 1992.

10) p. 140
"When you're making latkes," from *Iseult, We Are Barren*.

## GLOSSARY

p. 8
*Bekanntmachungen*: (posted) announcements

p. 8
*Ortskommandant*: Nazi-appointed mayor

p. 11
*Judenfreundlich*: Jew-friendly

p. 12
*Kulturkammer*: a Nazi organisation of which all cultural workers were obliged to be a member. It instructed its members to supply personal information, and obliged them to comply with its rules.

p. 13
SD, short for *Sicherheitsdienst*: Security Service

p. 14
*Polizeiliches Durchgangslager*: transit camp, run by special police

p. 18
*Gestapo*, short for *Geheime Staatspolizei*: Secret State Police

p. 51
*Glaubst du das, sie sagt sie hat keinen Mann!*: Can you believe it? She says she has no husband.

p. 52
*Wo ist die Mutti?*: Where's your mom?

p. 80
*Nun, was gibt's denn?*: Well, what's going on?

p. 85
*Grüne Polizei*: law enforcement troops (named for the colour of their uniforms)

p. 101
*Sie lachen noch wann die Russen kommen!*: You'll still be laughing when the Russians get here!

ACKNOWLEDGEMENTS

In 1982 I submitted about twenty "war poems," together with some sixty miscellaneous poems, to Mosaic Press, a publishing house that had expressed interest. I had it in mind that the war poems might be contained in one section. The editor, Ken Sherman, liked the war poems, but did not like the idea of diluting their message by adding unrelated text and asked me to write more poems. This proved a problem because I felt, at that time, that I had said all I wanted to say. In the event, I was wrong, but that's another story. Ken Sherman then hit upon a brilliant solution: could I write prose connecting pieces to fill in the background to the poems. This worked very well, and *Precautions Against Death* (Mosaic Press, Oakville, 1983) was the result. I want to thank Ken sincerely, both for the idea, and for editing the resulting text with patience and sensitivity.

The next version of the story was a translation into Dutch, *Vijfenvijftig sokken* (De Harmonie, Amsterdam, 1984). I embarked upon this venture with trepidation, as by this time it had been 30 years since I had lived in Holland, and my Dutch, though accurate enough, was distinctly behind the times. The publisher asked the prominent Dutch poet Judith Herzberg to have a look at the manuscript. To my great good fortune she consented. She had been in hiding herself during the Nazi occupation and responded to the story, told from the point of view of a "bystander," for want of a better word. Thanks to her insight and talent, her suggestions strengthened and improved both the content and the style of the text, and corrected several facts I had misremembered. Needless to say, these changes and corrections were retained in the present version, and I want to thank Judith warmly for her invaluable help.

One of the things that came clear after *Precautions* was sent into the world was that I hadn't told my readers enough. What else happened? How did these people fare in the end? Much happens in 20 years, and this new version of the book, *A Safe House,* gives an expanded picture of our war-time family. My present editor, Allan Briesmaster, suggested ways in which a Coda might look back, not only over the 20 years since *Precautions* came out, but over the 60 years since the Nazi occupation ended. Fewer and fewer people alive then are present now, and their stories often die with them. Allan helped me to keep at least this story alive a little longer. His fastidious approach to editing and his tact and knowledge all came together in making our collaboration a pleasure, and I am deeply grateful to him.

I want to thank my children, Richard, Ted, Vivian, Cecilia, and Francis Moens, as well as their wives and husbands, and those of my grandchildren who have read the initial book, for their responses. They have helped me re-write obscure passages and have prompted me to finish the story. Special thanks go to Vivian, who took time out of her busy schedule to read the final draft of *A Safe House* and gave me her remarks (of which there were few, thanks to Allan).

One of my longstanding friends at York University, Professor Emeritus Clara Thomas, gave me positive feedback the moment she had read *Precautions* in 1984. Not only that, she made sure that the book came to the attention of the media, particularly Ken Adachi of the *Toronto Star* and William French of the *Globe and Mail,* both of whom reviewed it thoroughly. In addition, she taught the book for several years in her graduate seminar on Life Writing at York. When she recently heard that the story was to see a new edition, she made several suggestions, all of which have been gratefully accepted.

After a good long life, *Precautions* went out of print some 10 years ago, the fate of most books. When this came to the attention of my old friend Robert Priest, he took the trouble of contacting Maureen Whyte of Seraphim Editions on my behalf, but without my knowledge, and roused her interest in re-issuing the revised and expanded version you now have in your hands. I am grateful to both Robert and Maureen for their role in bringing the book back in print.

Finally I would like to thank all my friends and colleagues at the Bohemian Embassy writers' group (later called Phoenix) who were present when the first poems in this book were being constructed, and who gave me encouragement, and sometimes hard times. I leave it to them to see if these hard times, in particular, have made a difference. Most of all, though, I want to thank them for their continuing friendship.

*Maria Jacobs*
*Toronto, 4 January 2005*

MARIA JACOBS was born as Marja Schröder in the Netherlands. She lived in Amersfoort, a medium-size city in the heart of the country. Her family became actively involved in the concealment and care of Jews sought by the Germans in occupied Holland. In the mid-fifties she came to North America with her young husband Peter Moens. Since then she has lived in New York and Toronto, borne three sons and two daughters, and obtained a BA in mathematics and an MA in English. After this, for many years, she ran the *The Axle-tree Coffee House* in downtown Toronto, where poets and musicians met. She published a magazine, *Poetry Toronto,* for about a decade, wrote three books of poetry, and edited several anthologies. She was a member of the team of readers which screened the entries for the CBC Literary Competition conducted by Robert Weaver for over twenty years. With her friend and fellow-poet Heather Cadsby, she founded the publishing house of Wolsak and Wynn in 1982, of which she is presently the publisher and sole proprietor. She lives in the Beaches area of Toronto with two handsome cats, Soot and Il Tigretto.